SPARK YOUR *CAREER* *in*

FASHION

*by Angie Wojak and
Marianne Hudz*

**SPARK
NOTES**

Spark Publishing
A Division of Barnes & Noble
120 Fifth Avenue
New York, NY 10011
www.sparknotes.com

Library of Congress Cataloging-in-Publication Data

Wojak, Angie.
 Spark your career in fashion / written by Angie Wojak and Marianne Hudz.
    p. cm.—(Spark your career)
 Includes bibliographical references and index.
 ISBN-13: 978-1-4114-9811-2 (alk. paper)
 ISBN-10: 1-4114-9811-9 (alk. paper)
 1. Fashion—Vocational guidance. 2. Clothing trade—Vocational guidance. I. Hudz,
Marianne. II. Title.

TT507.W54 2007
746.9'2023—dc22

                                    2006100654

Please submit changes or report errors to www.sparknotes.com/errors.

Printed and bound in the United States.

10 9 8 7 6 5 4 3 2 1

CONTENTS

PART III: CAREER-PLANNING TOOLS

SPARK *YOUR* *in* CAREER

FASHION

FOREWORD

by Eugenia Kim

One day in January 1998, I went shopping in downtown Manhattan. I was a year out of college, jobless, and—having recently shaved my head because of a bad haircut—bald. To avoid being mistaken for the Dalai Lama, I put on the red, guinea-feathered hat I had recently made in a class at Parsons School of Design. That afternoon, several store-owners noticed my unique chapeau. By the end of the day, three boutiques made appointments to see my collection. The only problem was . . . I didn't have a collection! So I sat myself down and made two types of hats, in wild colors like lavender and electric blue. The next week, my designs were gracing the windows of a few downtown stores. By February, Barneys New York had placed its first order. Before I knew it, I was selling hats worldwide and counting such stylish stars as Jennifer Lopez, Madonna, and Gwyneth Paltrow among my devoted fans.

The beauty of fashion is that you're only successful if people are actually wearing your designs. I used to make hats that people would wear once and then display on their coffee table like some *objet d'art*. But now that I've learned what my customers actually want, I feel like I'm *really* succeeding. When everyone from the girl who sells me my alligator skin to my assistant's mom to Mary J. Blige wants my hats, that makes me feel good. My assistants keep telling me not to answer the customer service line myself, but I always do. I just like to know that people like my stuff!

I love fashion because it's both an art and a business. If you really want to make it in this field, you have to be multi-talented. You not only need to be creative but also understand things like branding, production, shipping, and marketing. So when you're interning and just starting out, keep your eyes and ears open no matter what you're doing, no matter how mundane it seems—you'll learn a lot by osmosis. Be willing to do anything: pack boxes, stuff envelopes, fill out purchasing orders—whatever they need you to do. Pay your dues, and you can reap plenty of sweet rewards later.

You've got to be ambitious and you've got to be tireless to make it in fashion. But once you're there, lucky you! You'll have a career that's creatively fulfilling, professionally satisfying, and a whole lot of fun. And how many people can say that?

Eugenia Kim
Designer
New York City, 2007

INTRODUCTION

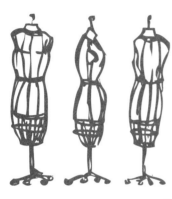

You already know that fashion is a major cultural force with the power to send trends and ideas rippling across the globe. But did you know how huge it really is? Apparel constitutes the fourth largest industry in the world. In 2004, U.S. clothing sales alone were over $170,000,000,000. Someone has to dress all 300 million Americans—why shouldn't that person be you?

The fashion industry offers a wide range of career paths to suit any personality or skill set. For every hot designer you read about in *Vogue*, there's a team of merchandisers, marketers, business analysts, and buyers helping to get that product out of the stores and into people's closets. So whether you see yourself as the next Donna Karan or her financial planner, there's a place for you among the fashion-forward.

That doesn't mean that getting there will be easy. Breaking into the industry is as hard as fashion is fickle. If you've picked up this book, we know you've got dreams of dressing the nation in beautiful garments and hip accessories. The question is: How are you going to make yourself stand out from the thousands of other starry-eyed hopefuls so *your* dream is the one that actually becomes a reality? You work—and that work starts with this book.

Spark Your Career in Fashion will give you everything you need to make your big debut. You'll get a crash course in how the industry works, plus a description of all the major players. We'll clue you in on what to read to be totally up-to-date on industry happenings. Never written a résumé or cover letter before? Don't sweat it. We're here for you. We'll show you how to land a killer internship or the job of your dreams, and how you too can create a powerful network of professional contacts—even if the only person you know in fashion sells T-shirts out of the back of his truck.

If you land a job, though—scratch that. *When* you land a job, you have to be realistic about what working in fashion really means. Be prepared to put in long hours and keep that inner diva under wraps while you climb the ladder. But for those who are willing to put in the effort and the energy, an incredibly dynamic and exciting field awaits you. And we're going to get you there.

TOP 10 SIGNS YOU WERE BORN TO WORK IN FASHION

1

You had to get a bigger mailbox to hold all your fashion magazine subscriptions.

2

You've memorized everything Tim Gunn ever said on *Project Runway*.

3

For your eighth birthday, you asked your mom for a Birkin bag.

4

You keep a videotape of your favorite red carpet moments, and you watch it when you're sad.

5

You customized your Nikes with a Louis Vuitton–print swoosh.

6

Your high school bio notebook was covered in doodles of Isabella Blow.

7

You actually pay attention to the swimsuits in the *Sports Illustrated* swimsuit issue.

8

You have every piece from the Target Paul & Joe collaboration, the H&M Stella McCartney line, and the Nine West Vivienne Westwood collection.

9

You think Anna Wintour should run for president.

10

You don't follow fashion trends—you set them.

PART I: INDUSTRY SNAPSHOT

1

HOW IS THE INDUSTRY DIVIDED?

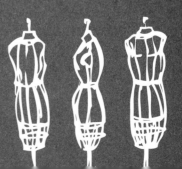

When most people think about the fashion industry, they imagine ads from *Vogue* and glittering gowns sashaying down the red carpet. High-end eveningwear is certainly an important part of the fashion world, but celebrities aren't the only ones who need clothes! There are opportunities available at every level of fashion, from million-dollar dresses and pricey bespoke suits all the way down to the T-shirts and accessories you snap up in bulk at your local mall. And don't forget—it's not just women who need to be dressed. Men, teenagers, and children buy clothing too, and *everyone* needs accessories to tie it all together. Read on for your road map to the big, beautiful world of fashion.

THE BREAKDOWN

Okay, so the fashion industry is huge. One way you can start to make sense of it all is to think about where clothes are sold and how much customers will pay for those clothes (known as the **price point**). The apparel industry is generally divided into the following five markets, in decreasing price order:

- **Couture**
- **Designer/Ready-to-Wear**
- **Bridge/Better**
- **Moderate**
- **Mass Market**

Resort collections, originally intended for vacationing jetsetters, usually evoke sun-dappled getaways with their light, breathable fabrics and casual, easy fits.

COUTURE

If you've got a cool $15,000 to $100,000 to spare, you too could be the proud owner of a terribly exclusive, custom-made haute couture gown. The term **haute couture** (French for "high fashion") refers to both a very select group of Paris fashion houses as well as to the clothes those houses produce. These one-of-a-kind garments, which often take 200 hours each to construct, are shown exclusively at the Paris Fashion Weeks in February and September.

Couture is probably the most misused term in fashion. In fact, a company cannot use the term *haute couture* unless they are officially recognized as such by the French Ministry of Industry, which will only approve a house for membership if it shows collections at least twice a year, features a minimum of 35 new designs per show, and employs at least 15 staff members. As of 2006, there were less than a dozen haute couture houses in existence, and the number has continued to dwindle because of the high cost of the design work and lavish biannual shows. These days, haute couture collections are largely used to create an aura of exclusivity and glamour around a given brand, which then sells lower-priced ready-to-wear lines, fragrances, and accessories that generate the income necessary to keep the entire line in business.

Many high-end designers have branched out into lucrative side products such as home décor, fragrances, and restaurants.

Fierce competition, work permits, language barriers, and current attitudes toward Americans make it almost impossible to find work in one of these houses, even as an intern, or *stagiaire*. Unless you know somebody (make that a *big* somebody), you'll have better luck starting your career in a more moderately priced company. Still, it's important to be familiar with the couture landscape, since it represents the pinnacle of the fashion world.

66 In couture there's no revolving door, so when an assistant or seamstress eventually leaves (which is rare) they often replace themselves with a friend or relative. You'll never see an advertisement for a couture job in the newspaper!"

—**Miguel Cruz,** Owner And Designer, Issa Miguel Cruz;
couture techniques professor, Parsons

The Players

In 2006, the official haute couture member list consisted of the following houses (including their founding year).

- **Adeline André** (1981), modeaparis.com/va/couturiers/aan
  After studying at the Ecole de Haute Couture in Paris, André worked for Christian Dior, Louis Feraud, and Castelbajac before starting her own line. Known for her languid, jewel-toned sheaths and her patented three-sleeve-hole garments, she presented her first haute couture collection in 1997.

- **Chanel** (1909), chanel.com
  Coco Chanel's legendary brand, which has become synonymous with good taste and understated elegance, is known for its suits, pearls, fragrances, and iconic "little black dress." Karl Lagerfeld became the lead designer for Chanel in 1983, bringing a sexy new edge to the brand.

- **Christian Dior** (1949), www.dior.com, johngalliano.com
  When Christian Dior began his namesake line, he was known for the femininity of his work. This legendary design house is now headed up by John Galliano, whose sexy, daring suits and bias-cut gowns— known for their superb tailoring—have reinvigorated the brand. Galliano also has his own ready-to-wear line.

- **Jean Paul Gaultier** (1976), www.jpgaultier.fr
  Gaultier's design work is inspired by art, film, and fantasy. He's credited with redesigning underwear as outerwear: He created Madonna's famous studded cone bra for her 1990 Blonde Ambition tour. Gaultier also has a younger, sportier, and less expensive line, JPG, and has done extensive costume work for films.

- **Givenchy** (1952), www.givenchy.fr
  Givenchy's timeless styles have been worn by some of the world's most famous women, including the eternal style icon Audrey Hepburn. Riccardo Tisci now heads design at Givenchy, returning to the brand's romantic roots with chiffon dresses and embroidered furs.

- **Christian Lacroix** (1986), christian-lacroix.com
  Lacroix debuted his line in the mid-'80s, when his famous pouf skirt became all the rage. He makes sexy, irreverent, theatrical clothing, with special attention paid to details. Bright colors, contrasting geometric patterns, and unexpected silhouettes are common features in his work.

- **Jean-Louis Scherrer** (1962), modeaparis.com/va/couturiers/jls
  Scherrer worked for Dior, St. Laurent, and Feraud before starting his own house. Originally known for the sophisticated gowns he created for the Parisian and Arab elite, his work grew increasingly exaggerated, featuring huge pants, cuffs, and bows of satins and silks. The line is now designed by Stephane Rolland.

- **Dominic Sirop** (1996), dominiquesirop.com
  After working for Yves St. Laurent, Givenchy, and Hanae Mori, Sirop published two books on haute couture before starting his own house in 1996. After only a year, he was invited to join the Chambre Syndicale de la Haute Couture Parisienne, the professional union of haute couture houses. He opened a ready-to-wear line in 1998. His dresses are sophisticated, beautiful drapes of satin, silk, and chiffon.

- **Franck Sorbier** (1990), francksorbier.com
  Sorbier's designs are known for their gorgeous fabrics, refined details, and clean cuts. His work is very feminine, often utilizing hand-painted

textiles. Before starting his own line, Sorbier worked for several other designers, including Thierry Mugler.

- **Emanuel Ungaro** (1965), emanuelungaro.com
Once a student of Balenciaga, Ungaro learned to cut with precision and pay expert attention to detail. Ruffles, embroidery, and the use of a wide range of fabrics, prints, and textures set him apart. Peter Dundas now designs for the house, following Ungaro's retirement. Annual sales, which include men's shirts, accessories, cosmetics and several perfumes, exceed $700 million.

DESIGNER/READY-TO-WEAR

When you think of the trendsetting, expensive clothing celebrities fawn over during the big runway shows, you're thinking of designer fashions. The term **designer** refers to high-end work sold at a much higher price point than most labels, often exceeding $1,000 per piece, and typically sold in exclusive department stores and boutiques. Examples of designer fashion brands are Marc Jacobs, Narciso Rodriguez, and Carolina Herrera. Most aspiring young designers hope to work in this category because of the accolades, brand recognition, and cutting-edge fashions commonly associated with the designer market.

Ready-to-wear (or prêt-a-porter) refers to high-end fashions that, while shown on the runway like haute couture, are not one-of-a-kind and thus—while still very, very expensive—aren't as exorbitantly priced. That's why you'll sometimes see two celebs wearing the same gown in *Us Weekly* (*quelle horreur!*). Lots of high-end designers create ready-to-wear lines that earn them a lot more money than their couture work.

Ready-to-wear shows occur in February/March and again in September/October, in this order: New York, London, Milan, and Paris.

Personality Profile

Do these descriptions sound like you? If so, you'll probably feel right at home in the world of designer fashion.

- **You love the glamour associated with chic fashions, and you're totally into label status.** If there's nothing you crave more than being involved with the hottest labels and your soul would disintegrate if you had to create products for the masses or the malls, then high fashion is the place for you.

- **You have a sixth sense for emerging trends.** To be a successful, cutting-edge designer, you not only need to have laser-sharp trend awareness, you also need to be confident in your ability to sense and proclaim new trends long before the rest of the public is ready for them. Do you always have a sneaking suspicion that *ELLE* and *Vogue* are tapping your phone to get their fashion leads? Have you ever put together an outfit that was so out there, everyone in school stared at you in shock—until they started copying it for themselves? You've got to be a trendsetter to make it in this part of the industry.

- **You're okay with being a team player . . . for now.** In your first or second job, you'll need to be prepared to play a supporting role and squash your inner diva. There's going to be attitude to spare in the studio and a ton of drama since you'll be working for some of the biggest names—and egos—in the industry. Particularly when big personalities are involved, it's critical that you keep your head down and your eyes on your own work.

Job Culture

Every company has its own particular work culture, but at the designer level you can expect a few things to be true across the board.

- **You'll work long, long hours.** The important thing to remember about working in designer fashion is that it's hard work. Designers and their assistants often work 10- to 12-hour days on a regular basis. Every detail in a designer gown has to be just right, including lots of tailoring, hand beading, and embroidery. And when they're not actually working on clothing, designers spend the rest of their time shopping and closely observing the goings-on in the rest of the fashion world. No rest for the wicked—or the fashionable.

- **Deadlines are king.** Whether you work for a large or small design company, the stakes are high and the product must get designed, manufactured, and to the client on time. That means that there's a good amount of stress to deal with on a daily basis. When Fashion Week approaches, the pace gets hectic for all departments. The design team usually works through lunch and into the night (sometimes even spilling over into the weekends) and generally gets by on a minimum amount of sleep. And as soon as Fashion Week is over, there's very little time before the whole company heads back to the drawing board, planning out the collection for two seasons ahead.

66 Working in a small, high-end designer studio, you need to be ready to pick up anything at any time because tasks aren't compartmentalized: You could be cutting silk at 3 A.M. and then be in charge of feeding the models at the fashion show the next day. I worked the longest hours I've ever worked for anyone when I was at a designer-level company."

—**Nami Payackapan,** Freelance Designer

- **Benefits? Oh, we've got benefits.** Most designer-level firms offer health insurance and vacation time to their employees. The larger the firm, the more extensive these benefits are (including retirement accounts). Smaller companies with just a handful of full-time staffers may offer more limited packages than a big company, or they may not offer benefits at all.

- **You'll be expected to match the brand.** Fashion people—surprise, surprise—care about the way they look. Fashion companies care about they way they look too, which means that your work environment will probably reflect your brand's aesthetic. At Calvin Klein, you can expect employees to sport a Klein-esque wardrobe of sleek, black, understated clothing and the workspace to appear clean and unruffled. Over at Narciso Rodriguez, the dress code will likely be more easygoing but still very hip. At most companies, the dress code for designers is relatively casual, so even at the designer level, jeans and sneaks are usually appropriate office attire. If you come to work in a suit, people will probably think you have a job interview later. Merchandisers and other business-side folks, however, will be expected to dress a bit more professionally.

The Major Players

The list of designer labels keeps growing every year. Here are some of the standard-bearers in the category (and the years they started their own houses).

- **Nicolas Ghesquiere for Balenciaga** (1995), balenciaga.com
  Ghesquiere's beautifully draped jersey dresses and severe tailoring helped revitalize Balenciaga's line. Born in 1971, Ghesquiere is seen as one of today's brightest young designers, and his work for Balenciaga graces such hip style icons as Kate Moss and Chloë Sevigny.

- **Dolce & Gabbana** (1985), dolcegabbana.com
  One of Italy's most successful ready-to-wear lines, Dolce & Gabbana's motto is "sweet and sharp." D&G draws its inspiration from the romantic film stars of the '30s and '40s, 1950s' retro garments, and rock and roll. Its designs, ranging from sexy denim to chiffon gowns, debut during Milan's Fashion Week.

- **Gucci** (1932), gucci.com
  Gucci started out in the luxury leather goods market and is now famous for its sexy fashions and accessories, particularly loafers and handbags, which feature a signature gilded metal buckle. Now designed by Frida Giannini (who had the unenviable task of following in Tom Ford's footsteps), the brand is undergoing changes as it adjusts to the new lead designer's subtler aesthetic.

- **Marc Jacobs** (1984), marcjacobs.com
  Marc Jacobs designs many collections, including this, his own signature line, as well as Louis Vuitton's ready-to-wear collection. Jacobs is known as a trendsetter, swinging from ladylike glamour one minute to grunge the next. He's also an incredibly successful accessory

designer, having consistently created must-have bags every season. He's a particular favorite among young, intellectual, urban women.

- **Donna Karan** (1985), donnakaran.com, dkny.com
  Donna Karan became famous for her collection of "seven easy pieces" that any woman could wear. One of these pieces was a body suit, which became a signature item for the brand. Over the years Karan has expanded her empire to include a lower-priced line called DKNY, and she continues to produce not only designer womenswear but also fragrances, eyewear, and menswear.

- **Michael Kors** (1981), michaelkors.com
  A favorite designer of many celebrities and an outspoken judge on *Project Runway*, Michael Kors is known for chic, luxurious American sportswear. He's yet another designer who's expanded his collection to include fragrances, sunglasses, and swimwear.

- **Ralph Lauren** (1968), polo.com
  With his decidedly American take on casual sportswear, Lauren made his mark reinterpreting menswear for women, giving pleated trousers and winged collars a feminine touch. Lauren's strong brand name extends to several other lines at various price points, such as Purple Label, Polo, Lauren by Ralph Lauren, and even a line of paints under Ralph Lauren Home.

- **Prada** (1985), prada.com
  This Italian luxury leather goods brand (which dates back to 1913) was reinvigorated by Miuccia Prada, founder Mario Prada's granddaughter, who took the reins as lead designer in 1985 and introduced the ready-to-wear line in 1989. *Refined*, *precise*, and *subtle* are all words that describe the Prada aesthetic.

- **Narciso Rodriguez** (1997), narcisorodriguez.com
  Narciso Rodriguez's designs are modern, architectural, sleek, and sophisticated. He worked at Calvin Klein for many years, during which time he designed Caroline Bessette Kennedy's wedding dress.

- **Vera Wang** (1990), verawang.com

  Best known as a Paris-style bridal couturier and awards ceremony dresser, Wang's creations are elaborate events of beading, duchesse satin, and silk lace. Wang was a fashion editor at *Vogue* for many years before she turned her attention to design—out of frustration that she couldn't find a tasteful bridal gown for her own wedding. Wang recently launched a private label brand for Kohl's called Very Vera.

BRIDGE/BETTER

Bridge fashions are one step down in price and exclusivity from designer fashions. Bridge lines often include career wear and dresses made of fine materials, with prices usually ranging from $300 to $600 per piece. Ellen Tracy is an example of a bridge line.

Better typically refers to labels with a price point between $150 and $300. The design, cut, and fabrics are usually superior to those in the lower-priced lines. Some designers who have ready-to-wear designer lines also have secondary lines in the better category. For example, Marc by Marc Jacobs is a secondary line that sells at a much lower price point than Jacob's work for the Louis Vuitton collection, considered a designer line. You can buy a blazer from Marc by Marc Jacobs for as little as $250, while a blazer from Marc Jacobs for Louis Vuitton will set you back at least $1,000.

The trendy but affordable apparel designed for women in their 20s and 30s is often referred to as **contemporary** clothing. If you take a look in your closet, chances are that a lot of the clothes you own fall into this category, which is usually sold in malls, specialty shops, or department stores. Contemporary brands include BCBG, Guess?, Betsey Johnson, and Laundry by Shelli Segal.

Personality Profile

For those who want to work on products that are trendy but more accessible to the greater public than pricey designer clothing, working in bridge, better, and contemporary could be a good fit.

- **You're okay with creating clothing that fits into an existing brand's aesthetic.** If you want to work at a fashion-forward company but are comfortable with the idea of following prevailing trends rather than trailblazing new ones, you'll find this category to be a good compromise.

- **You like the idea of regular hours and benefits.** If you really aren't comfortable with the idea of having little or no health insurance and you find it reassuring to have a set schedule, this could be a good niche. Keep in mind that there will still be times when you'll be asked to work extra hours to meet deadlines.

- **You were built for speed and you don't buckle under pressure.** The work environment at this level is extremely fast paced. A typical day on the design team might consist of fittings, sketching, working on design concepts, and team meetings with other departments, such as production or merchandising. Plus, you're normally working on three seasons simultaneously. While opening the showroom for the spring market, you'll also be reviewing summer products and designing for the following fall. And since companies at this level move so much more product than their high-end brethren, the merchandisers, account executives, and production people are kept correspondingly busy, as well.

Job Culture

At this level, you'll gain great discipline regarding the development process, experience in a corporate setting, and excellent contacts and networking opportunities. You can also expect the following.

- **You'll work long, long hours.** Are you beginning to see a trend here? Yes, the hours in almost all areas of fashion are long. But with larger, more established companies, the hours won't be as crazy as they would be working for a small designer fashion label. You should expect, though, that you'll often be working 10+-hour days during crunch time.

- **You'll happily enjoy structure, benefits, and resources.** Many of the brands that fit into the bridge and better categories are relatively large and can therefore offer benefits such as paid vacation time and health insurance. Unlike small companies, they often have in-house resources such as knitting machines and strong, established vendor networks. Need 600 spools of $\frac{1}{4}''$ pink elastic? No problem!

- **Workplace or playground? You decide.** Work environments vary widely at the moderate level depending on the type of brand you work for and whether the company is owned by a large corporate parent. For example, at a trendy company like A/X, you might work in a big, open loft space in Chelsea where you're surrounded by lots of cool, hip young folks, with music blasting and inspirational photos plastered all over the walls. But at a company owned by a large, more staid firm, you might find yourself working in a cubicle, office, or within a large loft space where designers and merchandisers work at desks with no walls.

The Major Players

The following are just a few of the best-known companies in this price point.

- **BCBG,** bcbg.com
  The name stands for *Bon Chic, Bon Genre* (Good Style, Good Attitude) and the company was founded in Los Angeles by designer Max Azria. BCBG is sold both in its own stand-alone stores and in department stores. The styles are very young and trendy, and in recent years the company has added bridal wear and beauty products to its line.

- **Kenneth Cole Productions,** kennethcole.com
  Kenneth Cole started out as a shoe company but has since grown into a huge fashion house. The look is modern and urban, popular with both teenagers and adults. His Kenneth Cole Reaction line targets younger customers. Kenneth Cole has been very active in human rights and AIDS relief activities, and he is almost as

Hot young up-and-comers: Rodarte, 3.1 Phillip Lim, Derek Lam, Peter Som, Trovata, Doo.Ri, Jovovich-Hawk, Thakoon, and Ashley Verrier.

well known for the humor and humanity of his ads as he is for his clothing.

- **Guess?,** guess.com
Guess? was founded by French brothers Maurice and Paul Marciano, who wanted to combine the adventurous nature of the American West with European styling. Now an internationally recognized trendsetter, Guess? made its mark by redesigning jeans with a stylish, sexy silhouette. They're known for producing edgy, provocative advertisements with images by some of the world's leading fashion photographers.

- **Betsey Johnson,** betseyjohnson.com
Radical and fun, Betsey's clothing pays homage to rock and roll. Mick Jagger, gypsies, motorcycles, and disco have all inspired her at one time or another. Her 2006 spring line was inspired by Brigitte Bardot in the 1960s. Betsey was one of the first designers to open a store on Los Angeles's Melrose Avenue.

- **Anne Klein,** anneklein.com
One of the most popular sportswear designers in America, Klein is known for classic lines, coordinated separates, and matching dresses and jackets. Customers, mainly successful businesswomen, mix and match her constructed jackets, pants, and accessories.

MODERATE

When you go to the mall, most of the clothing stores you see fall into the **moderate** category. Moderate fashions are typically mass marketed for the average consumer, are not equated with exclusivity as designer or bridge/better lines can be, and often use a **key item selling strategy.** A single item of clothing can cost as little as $20 or as much as $120. Moderate labels include billion-dollar companies like the Gap, Eddie Bauer, and Pac Sun, all of which are **store brands** (i.e., brands that own their own stores). Other moderate store brands include Wet Seal and Strawberry.

In a **key item selling strategy,** merchandising teams choose a single item and build a sales campaign around it.

Department stores such as Macy's, Hecht's, Kaufman's, Nordstrom, and Saks Fifth Avenue also carry moderate fashions from designers like Liz Claiborne and Jones New York.

One company, six distinct brands

Gap Inc., which owns Gap, Banana Republic, and Old Navy, sells products at a variety of moderate price points and for a wide range of customers. Parents shop for their children at Baby Gap and Gap Kids stores. Gap stores have clothes for men and women from 15 to 50 years old. Old Navy serves the same customers, but their clothing is less expensive. The primary customer for the Banana Republic brand is in his or her 20s and 30s, and the clothing sells at a higher price point than at the Gap. In 2005, Gap Inc. introduced a new brand, Forth & Towne, to appeal to women over 35 years old. One company, six brands, and enough clothes for the whole family!

Personality Type

Everything in moderation—that's the key idea at this level. Read on to see if your future lies in the moderate category.

- **You're creative and love fashion, but you also like the security of a steady paycheck.** Most large companies in the moderate category are very structured. You'll always know when your paycheck is on its way, and you can rest assured that there will be a set process for having your performance reviewed annually, along with regular salary increases.

- **You're okay with not being the center of attention.** You'll be working as part of a large team and have to be able to get along with lots of different personalities. If you dream of being Tom Ford, glorious master of your own design empire, you'll need to check your ego at the door. There will be opinions coming at you from *all* departments, so you have to be able to listen to other people's opinions and be flexible.

- **You don't need to create edgy, new designs to feel fulfilled in your work.** Working in moderate fashion calls for design work that supports an established brand and that will appeal to the average customer who shops at this price point. You will also be expected to create things based on past successes. For example, if you're designing for Banana Republic, you won't be able to indulge your dreams of creating a feathered, hot-pink miniskirt—you'll have to keep that one for your personal sketchbook. The good news is you can introduce your customer to fashion-forward trends by creatively integrating them into your brand's existing identity. The typical BR shopper, for example, might adore a hot-pink miniskirt if it were done in a sensible khaki.

Job Culture

Moderate-level companies tend to be more corporate than those at the higher end, though that doesn't necessarily mean they're stuffy. Across the category, you can expect to find the following.

- **You'll enjoy a great benefits package.** Most large, moderate brands provide great healthcare coverage, dental insurance, and life insurance. Companies generally offer stock purchase plans and retirement packages after a year, often matching employee contributions up to a percentage of the employee's annual earnings. These large companies typically offer professional development classes, online learning tools, and tuition reimbursement if you want to further your education. Most important, large companies provide a career ladder, allowing you to advance within the company's structure as well as giving you the opportunity to change directions and departments (from merchandising to technical design to product development to production).

- **You'll work long hours . . . but not insanely long ones.** You'll often work very long hours, as much as 10 or more each day. Sometimes, the larger the company, the more structure and support staff will be in place to support the workload. For example, larger companies have whole departments for fabric research and development, which save the design team lots of time. In the next chapter we'll get into the pros and cons of working for a large vs. a small label.

- **Every day is casual Friday.** The dress code at most moderate fashion companies is business casual. There's usually a lot of buzzing around since everyone is constantly busy. People can usually be found in meetings, working in their personal cubicles, or collaborating in the design studio for the next presentation. The décor tends to be standard office fare, with lots of room for samples and lots of table space for gathering around presentations. Unlike most offices, though, you can expect to see lots of sketches and inspirational photographs pinned to the walls.

The Major Players

Most moderate brands will be familiar to you from your local mall. Some of the most prominent brands in this category include the following.

- **Abercrombie & Fitch,** abercrombie.com
  Abercrombie is known for hip, preppy fashions—think sexy Ivy Leaguers—as well as for its racy, controversy-courting catalogs. Based in Columbus, Ohio, Abercrombie had annual sales of over a billion dollars in 2004. Abercrombie has two subsidiary brands: Hollister (hollisterco.com), a West Coast–inspired brand for the high school market, and Ruehl 925 (ruehl.com), a more sophisticated line for the post-college set.

- **Liz Claiborne,** lizclaiborne.com
  Liz Claiborne is an enormous company that produces brands as diverse as C & C California, Dana Buchman, Ellen Tracy, Enyce, Juicy Couture, and Lucky Brand. Liz Claiborne also holds licensing agreements with many major companies and produces products for DKNY Jeans and Kenneth Cole jewelry.

- **Diesel,** www.diesel.com
  Diesel is an Italian-based company that's been around since 1978. Known as much for its sexy ads as for its clothing and accessories, Diesel positions itself as a hot, youth-oriented brand. Its industrial-looking denim line is both extensive and fairly pricey. DieselStyleLab is an even pricier, more fashion-forward offshoot of the brand.

- **Tommy Hilfiger,** tommy.com
  Known for his classic, preppy style, Tommy Hilfiger's brand exploded in the 1990s and grew into an empire. His name now appears on everything from dishtowels to sunglasses. Hilfiger won the CFDA menswear design award in 1995 and recently purchased the Karl Lagerfeld brand.

- **Jones New York,** jonesnewyork.com
  Jones New York is a multi-brand apparel, footwear, and costume jewelry group whose holdings include four Jones NY brands: AK Anne Klein, Nine West, l.e.i. jeans, and Evan-Picone.

- **The Limited,** limitedbrands.com
  Begun in 1963 as a single store for women's apparel, The Limited has expanded into 3,700 specialty stores and a great catalog/Internet business. Personal care, beauty, and lingerie brands include Victoria's Secret, Express, Bath & Body Works, The White Barn Candle Company, and Henri Bendel.

- **Pac Sun,** pacsun.com
  Pacific Sunwear began as a surf and skate retailer and has now expanded into a million-dollar company whose stores sell the signature Pac Sun label in addition to many others. Its focus is on active clothing, footwear, and accessories for teens and young adults.

MASS MARKET

Everyone's got that five-dollar T-shirt from H&M that they've worn to death while ignoring a whole closet full of pricier purchases. **Mass market** refers to clothing that generally costs less than $50 per piece. This category includes clothing sold in the mega-retailers Wal-Mart and Target as well as lower-end departments stores, such as Sears. Forever 21 and Old Navy are two popular budget store brands.

Personality Profile

Ready to give it to the masses? Read on to see if the following descriptions apply to you.

- **You're perfectly happy working as part of a team.** If there's any place that screams, "No divas need apply!" this is it. At mass retailers you'll be expected to perform as part of a team. You'll crank out tons of work because the stores carry lots of merchandise. The teams tend to be closely knit even if they're large, because designers rely on each other so heavily to get the job done.

- **You're a good communicator, which includes being a great listener.** To work for a budget retailer, it's important to know how to work in a team and how to present your ideas succinctly. Because decisions are made by large groups of designers, it's important to listen carefully to get feedback on your designs and where they need to be modified. Your note-taking skills will be valued!

- **You desire for artistic expression doesn't outweigh your desire to create clothes that the average person would wear.** You don't mind that you're not doing cutting-edge design work. You're happy making clothes for a targeted audience, and you can put yourself in your customer's shoes. In budget, perhaps more than any other category, the customer is king. If you like the thought of creating and selling wearable, democratic clothing, this might be a great place for you.

Job Culture

The best news about working for a budget retailer is that the work is steady and there's a lot of it. You can also expect the following from most companies at the budget level.

- **You'll have plenty of opportunities for advancement.** Working for a large company means a tremendous opportunity for advancement. While some candidates may fear getting lost in the machinery of a big company, there are actually tons of job opportunities for those who apply themselves.

- **You'll get to keep reasonably sane hours.** Large companies tend to limit the amount of long hours their employees put in, so you can actually manage to have a life outside of work. Novel concept, huh?

- **Excellent benefits will be part of the package.** Most budget retailers offer a 401(k), health benefits, paid vacation, and job training. Sometimes, there's even on-site childcare for working parents. Many of the largest companies are big contributors in their communities—next time you're in Minneapolis, take a look at some of the art on exhibit at Target headquarters.

66 I went from designing for A/X Armani Exchange to working for a mass-market line sold at a budget retail chain. I came to the new brand with a very 'designer' approach to sportswear—I was accustomed to being able to add details such as trims, prints, and special fabrics. But with a tighter budget I found that I often couldn't add pockets to T-shirts or buttons to the fly of a pair of jeans because that would raise the production costs too high. Working for a line at a lower price point can be a challenge since you have to be creative within a more limited budget, which ultimately affects your design decisions."

—**Erica Sewell,** former Fashion Designer; Assistant Director
Parsons Career Services

The Major Players

According to the U.S. Labor Department, two-thirds of fashion designers in 2004 were employed in either New York or California. But when you look at job opportunities in mass-market fashion, you'll notice that many opportunities are located in the Midwest and South. The bad news is that you will likely have to relocate to a city that is not New York or Los Angeles, the major epicenters of American fashion. The good news is that the cost of living is much lower in other cities and the lifestyle often far more relaxed. Here are some of the top retailers you might want to investigate.

- **Forever 21,** forever21.com
  A top retailer for trendy teen fashions, now in 145 locations in the United States. Quick turnaround means that stores are able to continuously refresh items on the floor. Clothing retails from under $8 to $40 per piece.

- **J.C. Penny,** jcpenny.com
  According to the Fortune 100, J.C. Penny is one of the nation's largest retail, catalog, and e-commerce businesses. In the apparel department, the focus is on affordable clothing for the whole family, especially women of all ages.

- **Kmart,** kmart.com

  With its recent purchase of Sears, Kmart has become the third-largest retailer in the United States (after Wal-Mart and Target). Its department stores carry clothing for women, men, children, and plus sizes. Martha Stewart, actress Jaclyn Smith (of TV's *Charlie's Angels*), and model Kathy Ireland have all designed and promoted fashion and housewares collections for Kmart.

- **Kohl's,** kohls.com

  Kohl's is one of America's fastest-growing retailers. Like Target and Kmart, the department stores sell apparel for the whole family. Exclusive labels for Kohl's include Daisy Fuentes and Candie's for women and Tony Hawk's boarding-influenced line for boys and young men. Kohl's core shoppers are married women buying for their homes and families. In 2006, Vera Wang signed on to design a lower-priced collection for Kohl's called Very Vera.

- **Mervyn's,** mervyns.com

  One of the few apparel companies with design facilities in Northern California, Mervyn's focus is on affordable, wearable fashion for the whole family. A laid-back California vibe permeates the whole company, and the corporate culture actively supports professional development and a healthy work/life balance.

- **Old Navy,** oldnavy.com

  Old Navy sells "affordable fashion for the whole family," meaning that its apparel is wearable, washable, and versatile. Clothing retails from $7 to $35 per piece. Old Navy is well known for its cheeky, retro-style commercials and print ads.

- **Target,** target.com

  Target broke the mold for mass-market retailers with its "Design for All" philosophy, bringing truly stylish fashion and product design to the American public at affordable rates. Noted designers such as Robert Graves and Isaac Mizrahi have ongoing relationships with Target, and other designers (Luella Bartley, Tara Jarmon) have done smaller, more limited collections with the giant retailer. Target's in-house designers all work in Minneapolis, Minnesota.

- **Wal-Mart,** walmart.com

  Wait, did I hear that right? Wal-Mart? Advertising in *Vogue*? Incredible, but true. As the world's largest retailer, Wal-Mart sells billions of dollars of everyday clothing every year.

The Internationals

An increasing number of moderate and mass-market European companies are beginning to seek out talented designers from the United States. Check out these hot global retailers.

- **H&M,** Sweden, hm.com

  This mass-market behemoth offers versatile, trendy separates for women, men, teens, and children, often priced under $20. H&M (Hennes & Mauritz) has been incredibly successful with a series of short-term private label collections, in which a very-high-end designer (Karl Lagerfeld, Viktor & Rolf) creates a limited run of designs to be sold in the stores at budget prices. Marketers have dubbed this trend *massclusivity* ("exclusivity for the masses"), and it's certainly been working: The New York flagship store sold out of the 2005 Stella McCartney line in around 15 minutes.

- **Topshop,** England, topshop.com

  In London, Topshop is as important an institution as Buckingham Palace. (Okay, maybe only to some people.) But celebrities and young, unknown fashionistas alike head to Topshop for the store's amazing selection of youthful, trendy, and relatively inexpensive pieces. Like H&M, Topshop often partners with high-end designers, including Hussein Chalayan and Sophia Kokosalaki.

- **Zara,** Spain, zara.com

  Zara designs trendy clothes for 20-something hipsters who ooze international style. They're known for their incredibly fast turnaround—Zara can put a collection from design to retail in about three weeks, making them unusually responsive to trends. Zara launches a mind-boggling 10,000 new designs a year, and in March 2006 they bypassed H&M to become Europe's largest clothing retailer, with 2,700 stores worldwide.

I'll have the house special, please

Private labels are fashion lines that large retailers manufacture and sell exclusively in their own stores. There are often sourcing and cost advantages through direct manufacturing that can be passed on to the consumer, which means that private label items can sell for 15 to 40 percent cheaper than similar national brands. In addition, retailers enjoy direct control over product development and marketing. Private labels can appear at almost any price point: Macy's has a moderately priced line called INC., while Bloomingdale's sells a better private label called Acqua. Recent years have seen a boom in mass-market private labels, such as Isaac Mizrahi's Target line and the George label by Wal-Mart.

DIVIDING THE INDUSTRY BY CATEGORY

Now that you know the types of fashion design businesses based on price point, let's talk about the different types of design specialization. Think about your ideal customer. Maybe you'd like to design the kind of clothes you and your friends would wear on a night out—or maybe you've always been crazy about knitting little sweaters for your nieces and nephews (and your *friends'* nieces and nephews . . . and your *neighbors'* nieces and nephews). Maybe you've always wanted to dress starlets on the red carpet, or tailor fabulous suits for Wall Street titans. Chances are, you're already familiar with some of the companies and magazines associated with your category—but if you want to get a leg up on the fashion competition, you've got to research, research, research.

Women's

If you're primarily interested in women's fashions (and most people interested in fashion are), you'll have to decide whether you want to focus on high-end eveningwear and dresses or on lower-level **sportswear** and career wear. Because this field is so competitive, you may need to work your way through mass merchants and large companies before being hired by a smaller, higher-end company. A smart career strategy is to secure an internship or sales job with a label that matches the price point and design aesthetic of the brand you ultimately hope to work for. For example, if you're dying to work with Ralph Lauren someday, try to land an internship there while also sending out résumés to Michael Kors, Calvin Klein, Tommy Hilfiger, and other like-minded companies.

To learn more about this category:

Read these magazines: *Women's Wear Daily, Harper's Bazaar, W,* and *Vogue*
- Check out these websites: style.com, elle.com
- Research these brands: Marc Jacobs, Donna Karan, Michael Kors, Ralph Lauren

Infants' and Children's

There's almost always a solid job market in children's apparel, since kids regularly outgrow their clothes. Also, as children grow they become aware of trends, meaning there's a constant need to generate new designs every season. Infants/babies is a separate specialty within children's apparel, and design lines often include blankets, crib sets, and room décor. Parents and grandparents are the real market for this category.

To learn more about this category:
- Read these magazines: *Child, American Baby, Cookie*
- Check out these websites: www.juniorfashion.co.uk, earnshaws.com
- Research these brands: Baby Gap, Baby Phat, Little Me, Oshkosh B'Gosh, Children's Place

Tweens' and Juniors'

The term *tween* is used to describe girls between 9 and 12. They typically like cute clothes, matched sets, denim, embellishments, and accessories. They may read *ELLEgirl* or *Teen Vogue* or *Seventeen,* and they're usually very group conscious. Limited Too, Gap, and Aeropostale might be their favorite stores. Juniors are girls in junior high and high school who typically want to dress stylishly but at a reasonable price point. Many mass marketers target this customer.

To learn more about this category:
- Read these magazines: *Seventeen, ELLEgirl, Teen Vogue*
- Check out these websites: earnshaws.com, alloy.com
- Research these brands: Rampage, XOXO, American Eagle, Forever 21, Delia's

---

Have you considered . . . ?

One market that's gone largely untapped is plus-size fashions— with over $30 million in sales in 2003, the market is growing twice as fast as the traditional retail market. Along with unpleasant stereotypes about overweight women, the muumuu is definitely *out*. If you're interested in this category, research brands like Torrid, Elisabeth, and Lane Bryant and check out *Figure* magazine.

Men's

Men are becoming increasingly fashion conscious, which means that designing for men has a whole new appeal than it did several years ago. There are many price points in men's fashion—from mass market all the way up to designer—and many opportunities for designers. There's less competition for jobs in menswear because most designers want to be designing for women, and fashion companies often scramble to find qualified designers.

To learn more about this category:
- Read these magazines: *GQ, Esquire, Details*

- Check out these websites: men.style.com, the *New York Times* Fashion and Style Section at nytimes.com
- Research these brands: John Varvatos, Duckie Brown, Helmut Lang, Raf Simons, John Bartlett

Surf/Skate/Ski

This multibillion-dollar industry was born on the beaches of California in the 1960s. Starting with the young men's market—the surfers and the skateboarders—it has expanded into the juniors market and has gone inland and national with skateboarders, snowboarders, and wakeboarders. The designs tend to be ultra hip, with lots of room for movement. Well-established companies such as OP (now owned by Warnaco), Billabong, Element, and Quiksilver/Roxy have been joined by newer ventures like Volcom, Vans, and Hurley.

Even if you don't skateboard, snowboard, or surf, you can still look (and design for) the part. But the more you participate in these extreme sports, the better you'll understand the customer, and the more likely you'll succeed in working for these edgy companies.

To learn more about this category:
- Read these books and magazines: *Skateboarding, Surfing, Outside, Let My People Go Surfing* (by Patagonia founder Yvon Chouinard)
- Check out these websites: surfingthemag.com, transworldsurf.com, skateboardiasc.org
- Research these brands: Quiksilver, Burton, The North Face, Element

Active Wear

Turn on your television and count the sports shows. Then count the number of logos you see from sportswear companies. Nike, Adidas, Puma, and Reebok. Each of these companies started with footwear but expanded into apparel for warm-ups, teams, and casual wear. Comfort, durability, and ease of care are critical. In addition, these companies use performance fabrics like neoprene and Gore-Tex. Some companies, like Eddie Bauer, The North Face, and Patagonia, focus on hikers, rock climbers, and more extreme sportsmen. And now that yoga has become a mainstream activity in the United States, a new subcategory is sprouting up, with yoga-wear companies like Nuala for Puma and PraNa for Liz Claiborne.

Participating in sports and living an active lifestyle are probably the best ways to become familiar with these companies. There's a good chance that you're interested in these companies because you already wear their clothes and shoes. So go ahead, get out there and play already!

To learn more about this category:

- Read these magazines: *Sports Illustrated*, *Runner's World*
- Check out these websites: espn.com, si.com
- Research these brands: Adidas, Nike, Patagonia, Puma

Denim

Americans wear a lot of denim. It's the one thing you can reliably find in all the closets in your house, from your older sister's trendy Diesels to your mother's dreaded, high-waisted mom jeans. Levi Strauss, who has been making denim since 1873, now sells $4 billion in product annually. Abercrombie and Fitch, which started as a clothing line for fishermen and hunters, expects to sell a billion dollars worth of jeans in 2006. Other companies that do a lot of work in denim include the Gap, American Eagle, and Lucky Brand. And don't forget the hot newer lines, including Hudson, 7 For All Mankind, and Citizens of Humanity.

To prepare for a career designing denim, you can start by experimenting with denim fabric. See how many ways you can dye, **distress,** embellish, wash, and otherwise alter an old pair of jeans. Also, go shopping! That's right, we hereby give you permission. The best way to understand this category is to get out there and see what's flying off the shelves and to regularly check out websites that sell hot new denim lines.

To learn more about this category:

- Read this magazine: *Women's Wear Daily* (specifically the weekly feature, "Denim Report")
- Check out these websites: cottoninc.com (Lifestyle Monitor Denim Issue), revolveclothing.com, shopbop.com
- Research these brands: Rogan, Diesel, Blue Cult

Intimates

Lingerie, bras, and other intimate apparel constitute a niche market, and there always seem to be design opportunities available. Intimates are a largely overlooked category, and because of that there are often more open jobs than qualified candidates. New construction technologies and shifting trends (such as thongs and boyshorts) have made this an area to watch.

If you're interested in designing intimates, you might consider getting an internship for either a lingerie company or a swimwear company, since much of the technology, materials, and construction practices are the same. You'll need to know how to sew with stretch jersey, elastic, and specialty trims. Check out lots and lots of swimsuits, and try to figure out what makes each one special and marketable.

To learn more about this category:
- Read these magazines: *Women's Wear Daily*, *Contours*, *Body*
- Check out these websites: cottoninc.com, underfashionclub.org
- Research these brands: Adam + Eve, Vanity Fair, Natori, Victoria's Secret, Agent Provocateur

Accessories

Accessory design is the hottest job market for designers today, and it's booming like never before. Companies large and small are always calling design schools looking for handbag, watch, cold-weather accessory, jewelry, and shoe designers. Liz Claiborne has an entire New York City complex dedicated solely to accessories. For one thing, consumer demand tends to rise during a recession, since accessories allow shoppers to update their looks without having to buy a whole new wardrobe. Many of today's biggest fashion trends have come out of this market, pashminas and wooden necklaces being two recent examples.

To prepare, you should study leathers, construction, silhouettes, and trends. Many design schools offer classes in shoe design but may not have a full accessory design program. Developing good construction techniques is especially critical, since shoes and bags take a lot of punishment. To learn it all you'll definitely need to find a good internship so you can begin to understand construction, how to work with a factory, sourcing, and how to bring a product to market. It's also very important to learn how the costs of certain materials and construction methods will affect the production of an item. Even with large retail markups, the raw materials for accessories can be quite costly. The seaming on a bag, the quality of the material, and the processes used to treat the leather can drastically change the cost of producing a bag or shoe. Being able to determine how a different lining or buckle can be used to save money without resorting to cheaper leather could be the difference between getting a shoe made and seeing the design get scrapped.

To learn more about this category:

- Read these books and magazines: *Women's Wear Daily* (specifically the weekly feature, "Accessories Report"); *The Fairchild Encyclopedia of Fashion Accessories* (by Phyllis G. Tortora); *Accessories*
- Check out these websites: handbag.com, style.com ("Accessories Report")
- Research these brands: Coach, Kate Spade, Nine West, Fossil

2

WHAT KIND OF WORK COULD I DO?

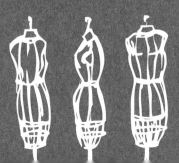

FROM THE DESIGNER'S MIND TO YOUR CLOSET IN 6 EASY STEPS

What happens before you put on your clothes in the morning? Easy, you say—someone makes it, and I buy it. Well, not exactly. Let's take a look at the life of a pair of jeans.

1

Designing the Product   The **merchandising team** begins by analyzing past sales and trends. Using that research, they decide what they want to show in the stores and present those ideas to the **design team,** who works with the merchandisers to solidify the season's styles. Designers then go on shopping trips to see what people are wearing and what's selling (and not selling) in their own stores and their competitors' stores. They come up with ideas about pockets, dyes, fit, length, belt loops, material, and zippers. Then the designer creates a design for the complete product, keeping in mind the target customer's age, sex, lifestyle, and income. The **production team** determines how to make the jeans, and the merchandisers help determine if it is a product that will sell at the projected price point.

2

Number Crunching   The **product developers** and production specialists calculate the cost of each item used in the garment and how much time it'll take to actually produce the jeans. Then the merchandisers estimate how much they think a customer would be willing to pay for the finished product. Unless the jeans can be produced for a fraction of the retail cost, chances are that something will have to change before the garment goes into production. Sometimes, the product developers need to find, or **source,** cheaper materials, production methods, or embellishments. Labor and materials are usually the most expensive components of any garment.

3

Constructing Samples   The **tech designers** put together a list of instructions so a sample can be made. Everything gets spelled out explicitly, all the way down to what kind of thread to use. After the sample is sewn it is put on a **fit model,** who models the garment so the design team and tech designers can check the fit before it goes to the manufacturer. Sometimes the pockets show up in the wrong place, or the jeans turn out too short, too baggy, or too tight. The designers make notes and adjustments. Several samples might be made before the pair of jeans is approved for production. If the jeans are denim, they may also go through **distressing**—they can be washed with rocks, dyed, frayed, or even burned to get the effect the designers want.

4

Buying   The company's **account executives** set up sample displays in **showrooms,** where they meet with **buyers.** These buyers, who represent various retailers, select fashions that they believe will sell well according to their store's typical customer taste level and upcoming hot trends. Companies that are manufacturers as well as retailers (such as Diesel) will hold meetings in which the sales force is introduced to the new lines and marketing strategies are discussed. Often, these meetings are held in large hotels and include several social events.

5

Production, Manufacturing, and Distribution   Once the jeans have been designed, the process is turned over to **production,** the people who will actually get the garments made on time, of the right quality, and at the right price. Designers stay involved, however, to make sure that the finished product reflects their initial concept. **Manufacturing** encompasses the cutting, sewing, finishing, and packaging of the garments. Often, the clothes you wear are manufactured overseas because the cost of labor is cheaper. **Distribution** is the process of getting the goods that were ordered by a store from the production site to a storage warehouse before finally shipping to the stores themselves.

6

Retail   Once the jeans have been designed, ordered by the buyer, and produced, they are shipped to the store, where the store manager decides where they will be displayed. The **visual merchandiser** arranges clothes on mannequins and in window displays. For some lines, the visual merchandisers at corporate headquarters determine product placement layouts and then send guidelines to the individual store managers and their employees, who arrange the displays according to their vision. Sales associates get briefed on the new clothing before hordes of hungry shoppers descend on the store to snap up the hottest new denim styles—without ever realizing just how many people it took to get those jeans there!

As you can see, there's more to fashion than making a quick, inspired sketch and turning it into a moneymaking piece of clothing that lands on magazine covers. Putting designs into production and then onto the sales floor is a process that involves dozens of experts in different fields, from sketch artists to graphic designers, accountants to business forecasters, buyers to advertising professionals. And the best news? There's plenty of room for new talent. Read on to learn more about the most common career paths in fashion.

DESIGN

If you've ever watched *Project Runway,* you've gotten a quick glimpse of the entire design process, set at blinding warp speed. In reality, it's a much longer, more involved operation. Designing involves finding inspiration for a garment, sketching ideas, selecting fabrics and finishes, creating a pattern, and finally producing a wearable, sellable garment for a target customer. Without the designer, there'd be no product. The entire fashion industry (not to mention style-hungry shoppers all around the world!) depends on these creative professionals to consistently develop new designs and trends.

66 I always tell my students, 'Fashion eats youth and beauty for lunch!' Because even though you need a big personality to be a designer, it really does come down to hard work and skill."

—**Miguel Cruz,** Owner And Designer, Issa Miguel Cruz; couture techniques professor, Parsons

Personality Profile

People who go into design usually love to sketch, are trend savvy, and enjoy shopping. They are capable of generating lots of ideas—sometimes 50 or more for a single outfit—are able to work with a team, and are able to work well under pressure. Your idea of a fashion designer might be Karl Lagerfeld barking orders at his assistants while constantly yelling for a fresh supply of fans, but most designers have to be a little more diplomatic and levelheaded than that. To be a successful designer, you should have the following qualities.

- **You can't seem to turn your brain off.** Designers have a seemingly endless fountain of fresh ideas. They get inspiration from everything: fabric, buildings, sex, food, music, art, and other designers. They can think of 10 ways to embellish a hem—in 10 minutes!

- **You're an artist, but also a craftsman.** Getting a customer to pick a garment off the rack to try it on is only half the sales job. If a garment doesn't fit well, the customer won't buy it. Designers—from the most senior directors all the way down to assistants in their first month on the job—must know how to look at the fit of a garment and adjust that fit for production. This takes not only a good eye but also attention to detail. Even though the production department will establish most of the technical specifications (unless you work in a very small design firm), you still need to have decent math skills and an ability to quickly estimate measurements without having to pull out your tape measure.

- **Your customers are your muses.** Designers need to intimately know the market they're designing for and should ideally enjoy and be inspired by their customers. Designers for children's shoes need to understand what toddlers can do (Velcro) and what they can't do (tie shoes). Surfwear designers know what surfers like, including types of performance fabrics, fasteners, and specific textile prints. If you're thinking about going into design, you should think carefully about what kinds of projects and people stimulate you.

- **You play well with others.** Most designers work in teams, and all designers have to work closely with other people, including overseas production offices, merchandisers, salespeople, photographers, and models. They have meetings with vendors, production managers, merchandise managers, marketers, accountants, sewers, and graphic artists. In addition to good people skills, designers must have good communication skills.

The Workplace

Who you calling small?

When people talk about smaller firms, they're usually referring to companies that are relatively young and independent, like Peter Som. But many small companies, such as Carolina Herrera, are more established.

The work environment in a design department generally depends on the size of the company (that is, the number of designers it employs, not necessarily the volume of business). Large companies hire as many as 50 designers, medium companies hire 10 to 30 designers, and small companies as few as 1 or 2 designers, who work closely with the company owner.

LARGE- TO MEDIUM-SIZE COMPANIES

Most entry-level jobs in design are found at large brand companies, such as the Gap, Tommy Hilfiger, and Ralph Lauren.

Larger companies are often more corporate and structured than their smaller counterparts, which means you may not get to express your creative side as often or as broadly as you might like. At the entry level, for example, you might be hired as the assistant designer for women's sweaters, or as the assistant designer for men's bottoms (get your mind out of the gutter—that means shorts and trousers). If your job title is "assistant designer, women's bottoms" for a large denim company, you'll work on sketches and research fabric for jeans, cropped pants, and shorts—but no sweaters, jackets, hats, or shoes. Also, when you work for a large company all your designs must appeal to a large audience. You might come up with a pocket that you adore, but unless both the senior designer and the merchandisers agree with you, your idea might never make it onto the shelves. You'll probably work within a larger team of designers to create complementary lines each season, ensuring that your cargo pants go with his knit tops and her safari-style shirtdresses.

The upside to working for a large company is literally up: up the ladder to more opportunities. Because of the size of these companies, there are many more jobs to be filled than at smaller firms. Often, an assistant designer can get promoted to associate designer within a few short years of being hired. Staying with a large company can mean moving around to many design areas—gaining experience in sportswear, denim, children's wear, etc.—and eventually heading a design team. Another advantage of working for a large company is, ironically, the corporate structure. Many of the largest firms have paid vacation time and profit sharing or retirement programs. Target, for example, has a policy in which any employee at its Minneapolis headquarters can ask any other employee for advice. The second floor has an entire area devoted to small-group conversations: It looks more like a hotel lobby than a meeting space.

SMALL COMPANIES

Smaller labels often attract more individualistic, creative designers because there's generally more room for expression and broader responsibilities. Designers at small labels often design several pieces for the same outfit. That's because, unlike at a large firm where you'd focus on just tops or accessories, you'll likely be responsible for creating a whole look. You'll have an opportunity to examine the inner workings of the business and get a bird's-eye view of the whole operation, not to mention that you'll probably also get to interact more directly with the lead designer. Small companies can often feel more like a family than a corporation, so if you're shy or you feel like your voice often gets lost in a big room, a smaller team might be for you.

Another thing to consider about working for a small company is that with great responsibility comes . . . well, great responsibility. Your role in the company is even more vital to the product, so you may work even longer hours than someone at a larger, more structured firm. (Though most designers at companies of all sizes work far more than 40 hours a week.) Plus, at a smaller company, you'll take on lots of varied responsibilities: In addition to being the designer you may very well be the merchandiser, the cost analyst, and the person who oversees factory production of samples. Most small labels only hire designers with some experience, so you might have to wait a while before joining a small company. Finally, salaries for entry-level talent can be slightly lower at small firms.

66 Working at a small, high-designer label can offer you luxuries like extraordinary materials—double-faced silk satin at $80 a yard and cashmere suiting—but it's also very demanding because you work in such a small group that it can feel like you're married to your fellow designers. At a larger, more corporate company like a big sportswear business, you can do your own thing and not feel that everyone around you is completely absorbed in the fashion world. At the same time, they can be very strict about policies and boundaries, and it can seem more sterile and impersonal than a designer or couture brand. It's all about figuring out what's a good fit for your personality."

—**Nami Payackapan,** Freelance Designer

Brand vs. designer

When working for a design house such as Polo Ralph Lauren, Kate Spade, Marc Jacobs, or Giorgio Armani, there's a real, live person who owns that brand name. Therefore, as a designer or merchandiser in those companies you have to remember to check your ego at the door. It's not about your vision as much as it is about understanding what the house stands for. In all of the above-mentioned companies, the designer with his or her name on the shopping bags will approve all products before they're shown at market. When you work for a brand, such as J. Crew, Juicy Couture, or Adidas, you'll still be expected to meet a high level of consistency, but there won't be one person who can claim a private right to the company's design direction. In brand companies, the CEO is often the business strategist, while the director of design and the lead merchandiser are the creative and conceptual leaders, respectively. In brand houses and designer-driven houses, then, the design team will contribute very differently to the final product.

Salaries

Check out designsalaries.com to see typical pay scales in your area.

As of 2006, entry-level assistant designers earn approximately $35,000 a year, with benefits at large companies usually including health insurance and paid vacation. Pay is typically commensurate with talent and internship experience, often with additional pay for those who have degrees from accredited art schools with fashion programs. Also, designers who are willing to relocate to the Midwest are often given slightly higher entry-level salaries than their counterparts on the coasts. Large companies will often offer bonuses and stock options.

While entry-level assistant designers can enter the job market in the low- to mid-30s, there is often a quick salary jump as designers move up the ladder in large companies. An assistant designer can be promoted to an associate designer position in as little as one to two years and start making $50,000 to $60,000. According to the U.S. Bureau of Labor Statistics (2004 report), fashion designers earned an average salary of approximately $55,000 per year.

Senior designers can earn anywhere from $80,000 to well over $100,000. Keep in mind that if you have your eye on advancing at a large fashion company you'll have to complete a bachelor's degree (even if it's not in fashion design but in a related field).

Prospects

From tiny companies that employ a single designer to the huge discounters and mass merchants, the need for fashion designers is growing. This is partially because of population growth and partially because middle-income Americans are increasingly looking for clothing that is both affordable and stylish. Plus, the trend-hungry tween generation now has more disposable income than ever. Advancement prospects are excellent, especially at large companies. Some of the fastest-growing companies, including major retailer Target, are adding design jobs at all levels every year. Abercrombie's corporate and design staff went from 300 to 1,200 employees in five years! Because companies often prefer to promote from within, you can always benefit from joining a company undergoing a well-planned, rapid expansion.

There is usually less competition for jobs in menswear, accessory design, children's wear, and teen fashions. The majority of young designers want to work in women's design, which leaves a huge vacuum in other areas that companies are desperate to fill with talent. Children and teens constantly outgrow their clothes and are exceedingly trend conscious, which means a constant, high demand for new youth designs—and, thus, new designers. Accessory design is probably the hottest, fastest-growing category where there are not nearly enough designers to fill all of the positions.

If you are determined to work in womenswear despite the heavier competition, there are many more opportunities in sportswear than in evening gowns. If the first thing you say when someone asks where you want to work is "Prada, Gucci, or LVMH," you're going to be disappointed, because their design teams are based in Europe and competition for openings is incredibly stiff. If you are open to working in sportswear and interested in designing for better, bridge, moderate, and budget lines, you will find lots of job opportunities. Larger companies move a much greater volume of product, so they need a constant supply of fresh ideas to fill their stores.

There's life beyond the coasts

If you're willing to move to another city, you may be more employable. Two-thirds of fashion designers are in Los Angeles and New York, but good jobs are also available in Ohio (Abercrombie & Fitch), Pennsylvania (Urban Outfitters), Massachusetts (J. Jill, Puma, and Reebok), Minnesota (Target), San Francisco (Old Navy and Levi's), Wisconsin (Kohl's), Orange County (Billabong, Quiksilver, Hurley, and Element), and Oregon (Adidas and Nike).

Job Titles

Although every fashion company is organized differently, these titles are fairly standard.

- **Vice President of Design**
  As a member of senior management, the vice president serves in a decision-making, business-oriented role, helping with strategic planning and operations. She works closely with the design, merchandising, and marketing teams to identify and meet profit goals. VPs (sometimes known as **brand managers**) have often been with the same company for many years, and lead the design teams in creating a consistent trend or style throughout the collection, brand, or category.

- **Senior Designer/Head Designer/Senior Product Manager**
  Senior designers help a company develop a consistent vision for all

fashions within a market segment (e.g., tweens or children's, but generally not both). At some companies, senior designers may focus even more narrowly (e.g., senior designer for men's bottoms at the Gap). Working several seasons ahead of market, they are constantly thinking about what clothes people will want in 12 to 18 months. Senior designers create original design concepts and work closely with their design teams to ensure that the final product fulfills the original concept, fits well, and is delivered on time and within budget. Strong communication skills, leadership ability, an expert knowledge of how garments fit, and an ability to multitask are critical. It generally takes between 6 to 10 years of experience at the designer level to be promoted to a senior designer position.

- **Designer**
  Designers are responsible for carrying out the design direction in their department (e.g., knit tops or boys' shorts) and for overseeing the **assistant** and **associate designers** on their team. It usually takes about three to five years at the associate level to be promoted to a full designer position and about one to three years to be promoted from assistant to associate designer.

- **Textile Designer**
  Do you dream in houndstooth and polka dots? If so, you might want to think about textile design. Textile designers create the images and patterns seen on fabrics, which means they've got their hands in everything from the curtains in your house to the clothes on your back. You'll need a great sense of color, knowledge of apparel production, excellent computer skills, and trend awareness.

- **Technical Designer**
  Technical designers are a crucial, in demand part of the design process, even though the title doesn't exactly scream "sexy" or "creative." The technical designer takes the fashion designer's concept and interprets that design so manufacturers can produce the garments correctly. They must have an innate understanding of garment construction and an ability to execute perfect flat sketches. Technical designers ensure that garments can be mass-produced

while maintaining shape and ease of movement. If you've ever seen a surfer in a full wetsuit, you'll notice it has a long strap to pull up the zipper in the back; that's because a technical designer figured out that that was the only way to zip it up.

The Ground Floor

The traditional entry-level position in fashion design is the assistant designer. Assistant designers take direction from their supervisors to help create the garments for a given season, known as a line. They sketch ideas for new products (though probably not until they've been on the job for at least 6 to 12 months) and help source fabrics, thread, and closures. Some assistants may be charged with designing small elements, such as embellishments and apparel graphics. Other responsibilities generally fall into the following categories.

- **Research.** Assistant designers often work on **mood boards** (collages of photos and sample fabrics), which are the initial inspirations developed by a design team. If your group is developing a line of bathing suits inspired by the jungle, for example, you might be asked to rent DVDs on life in the rain forest or to go to the library to make color copies from nature magazines. You might go to a nursery and look at exotic plants to see the shapes of leaves and the colors of tropical flowers. **Colorways** or **color stories**—the range of colors used in a season—evolve from the mood boards or are developed in tandem.

- **Shopping.** After the mood boards and color stories are discussed, an assistant designer is often sent shopping. You might be sent to buy competitors' clothes if they look similar to the bathing suits you'll be designing. You might buy a hammock to adapt the macramé into a cover-up, or some beads that look like those worn by indigenous people in the Amazon. You might buy hemp, cotton, or flax fabric, and you might experiment with dyeing clothes with beets, grass, or ground-up seed pods—all to get the right feel and color for your suits.

Some assistant designers do everything *but* design: They research, pick up fabrics and samples, and scout flea markets and eBay for new ideas.

- **Production.** The fun of shopping and sketching is balanced by the often tedious details of production. Once a design has been approved, it must be readied for production. An assistant designer or product developer is often saddled with the task of creating a bill of materials (**BOM**), which details items used in a garment, along with a reference number and supplier and price information. They'll also assemble **tech packs,** which explain to the factory each element needed for production. Since many large companies produce their garments overseas, tech packs must provide even the smallest details. Assistant designers must provide details including the amount of seam allowance, the distance from one button to the next, and the size of each individual stitch. Occasionally assistant designers travel to factories to see the garments in production, especially if there seem to be difficulties in getting the final garments just the way the design team expects them. (This usually happens at smaller companies, when more senior designers don't want to bother with the hassle of traveling.)

Where you enter the field of fashion design depends largely on your education. Many companies now require a bachelor's degree (BA or BFA) before they'll hire you at the assistant designer level. A degree in fashion design is ideal, but there are artists and designers from related fields who have found success in the industry. (Tom Ford studied architecture!) On rare occasions, highly talented or experienced new graduates are hired as associate designers.

If you don't have a bachelor's degree but *do* have a good portfolio and an associate degree or even a certificate in design from an accredited fashion school, you may get work as a design assistant. But wait a minute—assistant designer, design assistant; it's all tomato, to*mah*to, right? Well, not exactly. Design assistants are generally a step below assistant designers in terms of pay, rank, and duties. Students with AAS degrees from accredited art schools may advance into assistant designer positions after two or three years of hard work in the field. The size of the company and the breadth of their product will affect how fast you rise in the organization. If there are only three members of the design team, even if you wow them with your skills, you may never be the designer—at least, not at *that* company.

Tech packs include the BOM, spec sheets, construction details, technical flat sketches, and a blueprint.

Familiarity with a community with specific apparel needs can also be helpful. The founders of Quiksilver, for example, were surfers themselves.

MERCHANDISING

Merchandisers represent a perfect blend of creativity and commerce. They're responsible for interacting with the entire company—from design through production and sales—to determine the overall direction of the product line. They determine what kinds of products will sell well (Culottes? Sailor dresses? Jersey rompers?), how many items should be manufactured, and at what price those garments should be sold. Fashion merchandisers study trends and forecasts, analyze past sales, and calculate production costs.

Merchandisers wear many hats at once. As experts in design, product development, production, sales, and marketing, they make sure that all of those departments stay on schedule and stay true to the guiding theme or concept of the line. They keep close watch on sales trends and constantly work to produce garments and accessories that will feed into those trends.

Personality Profile

This field requires a college degree, preferably in business, fashion merchandising, or marketing. You must understand the competition, be acutely aware of fashion trends, and be able to anticipate what the customer wants before they even know they want it.

- **You love the thrill of being in charge.** If you're proactive and have good leadership and communication skills, merchandising could be a good fit. Working in this field is great if you like to have your fingers in a lot of pies and enjoy building strategies and managing large projects. Being skilled at seeing the big picture and how everything fits together is an important aspect of this job.

- **Bring on that math! It doesn't scare you.** This job calls for someone who is analytical, numbers oriented, and creative. You'll be continually called upon to analyze sales data and create profit and loss statements. Plus, it's up to you to figure out what's working and what's not working so that you can plan for future sales and adjust the product accordingly. Learn Excel now, as it's soon to become your best friend.

- **You know your Manolos from your Choos from your Louboutins**
  . . . A thorough knowledge of the industry is a must. If you love
  shopping in lots of stores before making a purchase and know the
  nuances that distinguish each brand, you'll enjoy this line of work,
  since you'll spend a lot of time researching your brand's competition.
  Caution: It's not enough to go shopping for yourself. First and
  foremost, you need to know your customers and their ages, spending
  and shopping habits, and taste levels.

- **You're a Zen master.** You must be able to handle stress and responsibility in this job because you'll be juggling lots of tasks simultaneously.
  At the same time you'll be expected to keep good relationships with
  the many professionals you work with on a daily basis.

66 A merchandiser needs to be really good with Excel and super detail
oriented. In a large company, a mistake can easily cost a couple thousand
dollars. Every day is a new challenge. Things are very intense, but it's
certainly appealing for someone who enjoys challenges, a dynamic environment, and interacting with people from all over the world. Just don't
expect it to always be glamorous!"

—**Viviana Kim**, Assistant Merchandiser
Jones Signature

The Workplace

Merchandising has no room for wallflowers. A merchandiser is like the
captain of a ship, operating cross-functionally and interacting with many
different departments to keep them all moving in the right direction. You
might spend the morning in the design lab reviewing the design team's
work, then go to the account sales department to analyze retail numbers,
then finish your day setting up the showroom with buyers and stylists.

Merchandisers have to be multitasking mavens, since they serve as
liaisons between design, production, and sales, ensuring the smooth flow
of information among these three areas. Plus, as a merchandiser you'll
work on three seasons at a time. You'll coordinate with retailers to make

sure the current season's clothes are selling well. At the same time, you'll work with factories to ensure the timely delivery of the season that's about to hit stores. Finally, you'll be checking in with the design lab, helping the design team edit next year's line.

Geographically, merchandising tends to be focused in fashion centers—usually large cities like New York and Los Angeles. You'll spend a lot of time in your office at the company's headquarters, but you'll also hit the road pretty regularly, checking out industry trade shows (to research things like new fabrics and construction techniques) while also soaking up culture more generally. From trends in the arts to political and economic factors, you have to keep your ears and eyes open for things that might affect your target customer's tastes and needs. For example, a few years ago New York's Metropolitan Museum of Art held a major exhibit celebrating the goddess. Fashion merchandisers noticed the buzz, and a year later Greco/Roman–inspired eveningwear was *everywhere,* with even flowing juniors' tops showing a decidedly classical influence. Designers created the garments, but merchandisers probably spotted the inspiration (and its profit potential) first.

Marketing or merchandising?

These terms are sometimes used interchangeably, but they're distinguished from one another by their level of involvement at the store level. Marketing focuses on getting the product to the actual customer and developing ads, catalogs, campaigns, and store events. Merchandising managers have more big-picture responsibilities, analyzing consumer trends and determining companywide policies for presenting the garments on the sales floor.

Prospects

With the recent mergers of the world's two largest department stores, May Company and Federated, many stores consolidated, which initially meant fewer jobs. Department stores are now restrategizing as they realize that they need more aggressive branding to differentiate themselves from all the other competitors in the field. For this, they often turn to the **private label.** Private label sounds like hush-hush black-market stuff, but it actually refers to goods manufactured exclusively for sale at a specific retailer. Private labels often represent less expensive alternatives to national brands and can greatly increase a given store's profit line. More labels means more opportunities for merchandisers who can develop, articulate, and execute those collections. Merchandising jobs are also on the rise because large retailers are increasingly spinning off into new market segments under new brands, such as American Eagle's Martin + Osa line, which seeks to expand AE's core young adult consumer base into the 25- to 40-year-old demographic.

Salaries

As an assistant merchandiser you will likely earn approximately $35,000 to $45,000, but salaries quickly go up with experience. In just a few years, an associate merchandiser can earn $50,000 per year. With more experience and a move into the title of merchandiser, $70,000 to $80,000 becomes a typical salary. Getting your MBA can be a smart career move and help you transition further up the career ladder, where you can earn over $100,000 as a merchandising manager or director.

Job Titles

- **Merchandising Director**
  This person is in charge of the company's end financial goal and makes sure that the merchandisers working underneath her meet their goals as well. She's also in charge of making sure that hot trends are addressed across the board. For example, if her market analysis demonstrates that sequins will be hot in the coming seasons, she might check that both the handbags and socks divisions are carrying items with glittery embellishments.

- **Division Merchandising Manager**
  A high-level executive position, the division merchandising manager works with his specific design department (such as men's tops or juniors' dresses) to develop correctly priced merchandise. He participates in business planning, budgeting, and setting sales targets. He also leads merchandising teams, including hiring, staff development, and performance evaluation.

- **Merchandiser**

  The merchandiser works with designers to develop the seasonal line plan (i.e., what's going to be sold to the retailers) and to create a design and development calendar. She makes sure that the product line comes in at the right price and that samples get to the sales department on time. In addition, she may oversee entry-level assistant merchandisers.

What's in a name?

When applying for a merchandising position, make sure you know exactly what it is you're applying for: In many retail companies, the title *merchandiser* refers to what is called a *buyer* in this book—that is, a person who selects and purchases garments wholesale from the manufacturer, to be sold in his company's stores.

The Ground Floor

Assistant merchandisers usually work in the same building as the design team, advertising execs, and sales force. You'll support your supervising merchandiser in creating **line sheets** (detailed reports listing products' wholesale costs, retail costs, colors, delivery dates, and so on). You'll also work with the sales executives and manage samples for both the showroom and for external accounts. Data entry for **style set-ups** (detail sheets on merchandise being carried, including color and pricing information) is a typical responsibility for an entry-level merchandiser. Many large retailers have entry-level merchandising trainee programs, which require a bachelor's degree.

PRODUCTION

Production is where fashion inspiration becomes reality. Once they're working on a large scale, designers can't make beautiful garments all by themselves: They need a whole team of creative people working with them, doing everything from making patterns to determining the cost of construction to making samples that will be sent to the manufacturers. These jobs might not seem as glamorous as those within other departments, but the salaries are often quite high for experienced professionals.

Jobs in this field fall roughly into two sub-fields: production management and manufacturing. **Manufacturing** encompasses the factory-based workers who assemble the garments for distribution. **Production management,** a more supervisory department, generally operates out of company headquarters and acts as a liaison between manufacturing and the design and merchandising teams.

Personality Profile

If you're good with your hands, love the satisfaction that comes with having a busy work life, are detail oriented, and like the idea of being part of a team, you might be a good match for apparel production.

- **They call you the Great Communicator.** Production people often have to be the bearers of bad news. It'll be your job to tell design that they can't make that beautiful trench coat exactly the way they want because the horn buttons and cashmere lining are too expensive. You have to work to earn the design team's trust, assuring them that you understand the design process and are trying to preserve their vision so they relent when you present them with alternative options. Sometimes you'll feel like a ping-pong ball bouncing between departments: Merchandising will want to sell that new polo shirt for $59, but design wants to use a special treated cotton that'll cost more than $59 alone. As the person who must force your coworkers into accepting reality, you'll often find yourself stuck in the middle of interdepartmental disagreements. Finally, you have to learn how to convey information and instructions clearly and concisely to your factories, often with overseas vendors for whom English is (at best) a second language.

- **You're not a spotlight hog.** Probably the number-one reason people don't check into these jobs is that they want to be part of the glamorous world they see in magazines like *Vogue*. But if you are okay with working behind the scenes and applying your skills to the technical side of the design process, you could enjoy a very satisfying career in production.

- **You're so quick and efficient, you're practically a well-oiled machine yourself.** This is not the job for someone who deliberates for hours on end. It's a job that demands you be decisive, detail oriented, terrific with follow-up, and good with time management. If you're a technical designer but have no patience with details, you could have a big mess on your hands when you approve measurements on that new pair of jeans and they come back with one leg shorter than the other.

66 Production and product development allow me to be creative, as I work with the design team to make their visions a reality. I balance that with the business-oriented work I do with the merchandising and finance departments and the challenge of finding manufacturing solutions with the factories. It's the ideal left-brain, right-brain collaboration."

—**Barbara Knapp,** Head of Production
Rogan LLC

Workplace

Production management employees generally work in the same office headquarters as the design and merchandising departments, although sometimes they're located in separate satellite offices. They'll often travel with the design team, especially if the company has an overseas office, and they'll sit in with the designers when samples are being created and discussed. Sometimes they'll visit factories, dye houses, and fabric mills. A good senior production person knows all of her factories and what they're capable of.

Although much manufacturing work happens overseas these days, there's still significant work being done in the United States. Manufacturing generally takes place in a warehouse-type setting, because of the number of garments being made and the number of people involved in making them. These workrooms usually have many stations, from cutting to sewing to pressing to packaging. Hours are usually standard but may be more than 40 hours a week right before a big delivery date.

Don't expect to see Anna Wintour stalking the factory floor. There isn't much glamour associated with this part of the industry, so if you're interested in the flashier elements of fashion you'll probably be disappointed here. But if you love seeing things done well and can take a quiet pride in contributing to the complicated process of making beautiful clothing, production just might be for you.

Salaries

The salary range for production jobs is pretty huge—from $20,000 to over $150,000. Generally, the lower the skill level and the less time on the job, the lower the wage. The least skilled workers—pattern graders and cutters—usually make in the $20,000 range. Sample makers can make up to $30,000, and a good patternmaker can make as much as $50,000.

Salaries can start in the low- to mid-$30,000s for production assistants (the entry-level position in production management), but if you advance to director of production you could earn over $150,000 a year.

Technical designers are always in demand. Their starting salaries are about $40,000, and within 7 to 10 years they can make over $150,000.

Prospects

This area of the fashion industry is relatively easy to break into, partially because manufacturing work, at least, involves more basic skills than design or business and partially because fewer people are drawn to these lower-profile positions. And since every season means that a huge amount of new apparel has to be constructed, there will always be a need for knowledgeable people in this field.

It can take many years to reach the top of the production management ladder, because the job requires such vast knowledge and expertise. If you'd like to be a product developer or production manager someday, the best place to start is as a production assistant at a small company, where production and product development are generally combined into a single process. People who have a good work ethic combined with technical skills and "soft" skills have the best chance of being promoted, because product management requires both manufacturing know-how and leadership ability. As in many parts of the fashion industry, you often have to switch companies to advance in this field, because it's rare that a position above you will open up at the exact same time you're ready to get promoted.

Advancement opportunities in manufacturing production, such as cutters and sample makers, tend to be more limited than those in production management. Job moves in these areas, which require much more basic skills, tend to be lateral, and salaries are also more limited. Many people who go into the manufacturing side of production are more interested in steady work than in advancement. Although much of this work has gone overseas to Asia and to Central America, the garment districts in New York and Los Angeles still have extensive job listings for these positions. In Los Angeles, pick up a copy of the *California Apparel News,* and in New York, *Women's Wear Daily (WWD).* Look for companies that do some or all of their production right near their design studios—these are likely to offer the best working conditions and chances for advancement. Because of new team-oriented modules, career advancement may be easier. Beginning as a cutter, patternmaker, or sewing machine operator, you could advance into production management, technical design, or quality control.

Job Titles

PRODUCTION MANAGEMENT

This department can go by many different names. Some companies call it *sourcing,* some call it simply *production,* and some refer to it as *manufacturing,* a holdover from the days when garment assembly mainly took place domestically and in conjunction with the other elements of production. As with any department, titles change from company to company.

Technical designers are sometimes filed under design and sometimes under production, although their basic duties—conducting fittings, doing flat sketches, and establishing tech packs for production—don't change.

- **Production Manager**

  The production manager supervises the entire garment production process. This job involves a significant amount of responsibility: ensuring that product development and delivery schedules are met, performing quality control and cost analysis, negotiating prices with vendors, and overseeing factory performance. Production managers also travel often, especially as more and more manufacturing takes place in overseas factories. Production managers might come from backgrounds in patternmaking, grading, or costing or start out as production assistants and progress into this role. A bachelor's degree in fashion is highly recommended, but a background in industrial engineering is also valuable.

- **Product Developer**

  If the designer is the visionary who dreams up the concept and the technical designer is the architect who translates that concept into workable blueprint, the product developer is the builder who takes that 2D document and turns it into a live garment. Product developers are problem solvers. They figure out how to realize the designer's vision within the scope of the merchandiser's budget, so they have to be creative when it comes to solving construction and costing puzzles. At the same time, product developers perform quality control, ensuring that garments are well-made enough that the warehouses don't get flooded with returns when buttons start popping off and zippers start jamming.

  In smaller companies, designers may handle product development duties, as well.

- **Patternmaker**

  A patternmaker takes the technical designer's sketches, flats, and drapes and interprets them into patterns used to construct both samples and retail-ready garments. A solid knowledge of computer-aided design (CAD) is an essential part of the job, as is an accurate knowledge of body proportions and sizes. With experience, patternmakers can become product managers or technical designers.

  ### Got an engineer's brain and a fashionista's heart?

  Think about becoming a **quality control engineer.** These professionals, who often come from a business background, ensure that the quality of garments being shipped to retailers meets certain standards. Salaries can exceed $100,000 with experience. Or you might consider becoming a **costing engineer,** who determines the total cost of manufacturing garments, from raw materials to labor, for the purpose of guiding design decisions and setting the final retail cost. Experienced costing engineers can earn between $50,000 and $80,000 a year.

MANUFACTURING

These positions may only call for a two-year degree rather than a full bachelor's, and some companies will count experience in lieu of education. Although most manufacturing jobs have moved overseas, there is still a small and vital demand for domestic workers from smaller, high-end brands, such as couture-quality lines like Bill Blass or Oscar de la Renta or the boutiques run by young designers launching their own lines.

- **Pattern Grader** and **Pattern Marker**
  Graders take the patternmaker's plan for a garment and translate it into different sizes, a task that requires excellent computer skills. *Markers* determine the best, most efficient ways to lay out a pattern on the fabric in order to reduce waste.

- **Sample Maker**
  A sample maker creates the first prototype of a designer's garment, usually out of an inexpensive material such as muslin. This work calls for excellent sewing and construction skills. Sample makers need to follow directions with great care. Often—make that *usually*— the samples will be sent back to the sample maker for corrections after the designer and technical designer conduct their fittings.

- **Cutter**
  Cutters cut out material that will then be sewn into garments by other team members. They need to have a good understanding of fabric as well as spatial relationships so that they can use the fabric most efficiently. The actual cutting is rarely done with scissors but with machines like electric saws or computerized cutting programs.

- **Sewing Machine Operator**
  Industrial sewing machines are not your mother's machines: They're faster, more powerful, and have many more capabilities. Sewing machine operators make up about one-third of all production workers, so there's often work available for someone with a few basic classes under his belt.

The Ground Floor

Assistant-level jobs in production and product development are a lot like any other entry-level job. You can expect a mountain of clerical work and more data entry than you can shake a stick at. You'll track and coordinate shipments, schedules, purchase orders, and correspondence. You'll also get out from behind your desk to open, pack, log, and send out cartons of samples. As you gain more experience and more respect from your bosses, you'll be given more authority to approve purchases and statistics on your supervisor's behalf. The key to advancing is being proactive: getting involved with fittings, staying on top of delivery deadlines, and offering creative solutions when a factory can't execute a shipment as planned. From production assistant, you'll rise to become a production associate, which can take about two years, and from there to product manager can take another two to three years. Making the leap to top-level management is where people skills—the ability to teach, lead, and delegate—comes into play, not to mention a healthy dose of luck and timing.

Most of the production work being done in the United States involves planning and supervision of the manufacturing process. You'll do a lot of CAD (computer-aided design) work for digital patternmaking and preplotting, but you won't be involved in much hands-on construction. Although limited on-the-job training is available, you should have a good handle on clothing construction, textiles, patternmaking, manufacturing production, sewing techniques, or tailoring to apply for these positions, in addition to familiarity with CAD programs. Community colleges, technical/trade colleges, and the continuing education departments of fashion schools offer plenty of classes that teach these skills.

Entry-level jobs in manufacturing require far less expertise than those in production management. Once you know how to operate an industrial sewing machine and have some familiarity with different fabrics and construction techniques, you can probably find work. The majority of manufacturing work in the United States is located in New York and Los Angeles.

The California
Market Center in
L.A. (california
marketcenter.com)
houses over 1,000
showrooms.

ACCOUNT EXECUTIVE TEAM

Account executives are the fashion company's salespeople. These business professionals generally work in **showrooms** that are set up like small stores, in which the next season's merchandise is displayed. There, the account executives help buyers from various retailers select items for their respective stores. For example, an account executive for the high-end denim line 7 For All Mankind will work with buyers from large department stores, such as Bloomingdale's, as well as buyers from smaller boutiques to determine which jeans will best meet the particular demands and tastes of the stores' customers. Account executives spend time making sure that buyers understand the benefits of each garment as well as the best way to display the merchandise in their stores.

Personality Profile

Account execs have to be salespeople who can successfully pitch a product as well as understand the market and their company's direct competitors. To enter this field you must have at least a bachelor's degree, preferably in fashion marketing or business. Here are a few important skills and personality traits that an aspiring account executive should have.

- **Your sock drawer is sorted by color, brand, and texture.** Account executives need to be analytical, methodical, and meticulous, because a lot of your job depends on your ability to track inventory and keep excellent records. In addition, anyone who wants to become an account exec needs a firm understanding of retail math and business.

- **You're no slouch when it comes to computers.** You'll spend a lot of your time managing spreadsheets, making projections, and writing reports, so you absolutely must have excellent computer skills. Excel and Word are essential, as is the ability to effectively use the Internet for research.

- **You can sell anything . . .** You've got a silver tongue and you love using it. Ten years ago you sold the hell out of those Girl Scout cookies, and now you're the top ticket-seller for your band and the top ad-seller for your newspaper. You can talk to people easily and quickly win their confidence. Any sales experience will be invaluable to you here.

- **. . . and gosh darn it, people like you.** Relationship building is a crucial aspect of this job. Buyers will come to rely on your advice—and therefore buy lots of products from you—if you prove that you can help them select garments that consistently sell well. To cultivate these strong, long-lasting relationships, you need to have excellent people skills in addition to your uncanny sense of market trends. You remember names and important details and have a way of making people trust you.

66 The most important thing is to know your numbers. Successful account executives are those who know what the buyer wants and what product is really going to sell—those skills are even more important than personality. Account sales can be a confrontational environment, so the more information you have about your product and your 'opponents,' the more effectively you can negotiate.

—Steve Lindner, Consultant to fashion companies including Donna Karan, Hugo Boss, Ermenegildo Zegna, and Escada

The Workplace

Account executives spend a lot of time with people and a lot of time with numbers. You'll spend a significant amount of time interacting with clients, but you'll also spend a lot of time at your desk poring over spreadsheets. In this job, every day is different, which means that you have to be able to think on your feet. You're always going to be checking that orders are completed properly, your buyers are happy, and the showroom looks terrific. This takes energy, focus, and a positive attitude.

The work can be particularly stressful around **market week,** when account execs walk clients through the showroom and introduce the products, using various financial reasons (such as past sales) to sell the vendor on certain garments. Even though it can be fun showing your

Senior-level account execs spend a lot of time on the road, sometimes as much as three weeks per month.

line, the company is most interested in how many orders you receive. It's a bottom-line business.

On the business side, fashion companies are really much like any other corporation in terms of structure, hierarchies, and workplace environment. Your workplace won't look like a typical cubicle field, though, because in addition to spreadsheets and computers, your showroom or office will be packed with clothing racks filled with samples. Keep in mind that, as an account exec, you're a businessperson. If you walk into the design studio you'll often see staffers wearing jeans and funky clothing, but if you work in the business, marketing, or public relations end, you'll be expected to dress somewhat more conservatively. (Business casual is usually acceptable.)

Salaries

An assistant account executive can expect to make $30,000 to $40,000 per year and can anticipate earning over $75,000 annually as an account executive. As a VP of sales, earnings can exceed $100,000 a year plus commission bonuses.

Prospects

Because the majority of people looking for entry-level jobs in fashion business want to go into merchandising or buying, the competition is less fierce for this particular career track. In addition, there are few companies that offer entry-level training programs for recent grads. Once you land that first sales job, though, your prospects for advancement are good because there are clear paths for working your way up the sales ladder, and promotions can come more quickly than in other fields. At the entry level, it takes about six months of showroom prep before you can start handling small accounts. Then, after you prove yourself in about a year and half to two years, you can get major accounts like department stores, such as Federated or Saks Fifth Avenue. Ultimately, your power lies in your relationships with the buyers. If you leave one company to go to a new company, you can write your own ticket in regard to salary if you've established relationships with key buyers in the industry and can bring your high-volume accounts with you.

Job Titles

The following are typical job titles in sales departments. Again, you'll notice that there are many similarities and overlaps in responsibility among these positions.

- **VP of Sales**
  The VP of sales plans the overall goals of the whole department (and for all stores served) and makes sure all account executives meet the sales plan. He or she looks at the big picture in terms of sales, planning, and goals.

- **Account Executive**
  Account execs are responsible for selling and financial account management for particular stores, driving account profitability, creating a sales plan for each store, monitoring retail performance, and working with merchandise coordinators and sales directors to improve sales performance at stores.

- **Assistant Account Executive**
  This entry-level position often calls for a bachelor's degree in marketing or business. Movement into an associate account executive position is the next step and involves trend and sales analysis to prepare account executives for market appointments and making sure orders get processed.

The Ground Floor

As an assistant account executive, your main responsibilities involve maintaining orders and financial forms for your company. Depending on the brand, you may also be charged with organizing and sending out samples to potential buyers. You'll also work in the showroom, guiding buyers around the merchandise and doing your best to make sure that they purchase your clothing in sufficient quantities to meet your company's financial plan. Assistants may also be put in charge of ensuring that inventory goes out on a timely basis. Recommending markdowns for buyers and gathering samples for buyers to place in their advertising photo shoots could also be part of your day-to-day responsibilities.

BUYING

Buyers provide the crucial link between the manufacturing company and the consumer. After the garment has been designed, produced, and marketed, a buyer steps in to bring the product into the store itself. When account executives display their company's merchandise in a showroom, buyers meet with them to select fashions they can sell in their stores at a healthy profit. Without this key member of the retail chain, stores could only carry private label brands.

Being a buyer doesn't mean you just get to shop all day, though. Buyers also have to analyze sales and plan inventory levels and markdowns. It's their job to predict what consumers will buy and how much product their stores can expect to move.

Personality Profile

A buyer must have an excellent eye for trends, love fashion and shopping, be open to traveling, and be very budget conscious and good with math. This is not a job for shy wallflowers, as buyers are constantly on the go, meeting account executives, hunting down the next hot trends, and finding the best buys.

- **You're no crybaby.** You must be aggressive, firm, and a great negotiator. People are going to yell at you sometimes, like when a shipment you've arranged arrives late and throws off sales numbers. You can't take things personally.

- **You knew blue was going to be the new black a year before everyone else—and that brown was on the horizon.** Buyers need to have excellent, even prescient, trend awareness. You not only need to know what's hot now, you need to know what's going to be hot one to two years down the road, since it's your job to anticipate—and in many ways, shape—consumer shopping trends. Buyers also need to have a great understanding of their target customer in order to buy products that will sell well. If you're a buyer for Mervyn's, for example, you need to appreciate that your core shoppers are looking for casual California style, which means no dry-clean-only fabrics and lots of colorful, breathable clothing. If boleros are the new "it" item this season, you might need to find a more conservative variation on the trend, such as a cropped jacket in khaki or denim.

- **Forget lemonade stands—when you were a kid, you ran a vintage clothing boutique off your front lawn.** Buyers should have an entrepreneurial spirit, since the job can often feel like running your own small company. The retailer gives you a lump sum per season and it's up to you to figure out how to spend that money and fill the racks with trendy clothes that'll sell like hotcakes. You and your immediate team will work fairly independently, although you'll go to your supervisor for general guidance and coordinate themes with other departments. (Is this season all about the Wild West? You'll be coordinating with men's, women's, and accessories to make sure you all incorporate a Southwestern palette and some distressed leather.) Education in strategic planning, business, and retail math is essential. You must also be able to negotiate with wholesalers and feel comfortable with a high level of responsibility and stress.

The Workplace

Being a buyer means very long hours, especially during **market weeks,** when buyers visit designers' showrooms and place orders. Buyers also go to retail trade shows, where manufacturers set up displays of their garments in large convention centers or auditoriums. Certain market segments have their own shows—for example, the action sports and youth lifestyle show sponsored by Action Sports Retailer (asrbiz.com). (Sorry, these shows are not open to the public.) During these shows, buyers get to meet and work with new, up-and-coming companies—meetings which can often last late into the night, segueing into a more partylike atmosphere. When they're not at the shows or in the showrooms, buyers are busy tracking sales and making sure deliveries occur on time. On Monday mornings, buyers crunch numbers from the past week to create sales reports for senior management.

You can expect a relatively high level of stress in this field, since buyers are ultimately responsible for store profits. As with any high-stress job, you'll have to handle the emotional ups and downs. When you buy hundreds of tiaras thinking they're sure to be the hot new daytime accessory and they end up languishing in the storeroom, you have to deal with low sales and an unhappy boss. This can often take nerves of steel and a flawless poker face. If you have a tendency to buckle under pressure, consider a different part of the industry. On the upside, though, sometimes you'll be the one to spot, purchase, and sell through the hot item of the season, which can provide a huge rush and a truly tangible feeling of accomplishment.

❝❝ As an assistant buyer, the biggest surprise was how financial the job ended up being. I soon realized that being a buyer meant running a business. Market appointments were more about finding styles that would be profitable than finding the styles I liked the most. It's a great job for anyone who seeks a future in running a fashion-based business from top to bottom. But I do think it's important to understand that being a buyer is 90 percent about profit and only 10 percent about fashion."

—**Angela Tsuei,** former Assistant Buyer
Lord & Taylor

Salaries

Entry-level assistant buyers earn in the mid-$30s to mid-$40s. Associate buyers can earn $50,000 to 70,000 a year, and buyers with five or more years' experience can earn over $100,000. A good portion of a buyer's income relates directly to sales and comes in the form of incentives and bonuses. If you make your sales target and your **gross margin,** you get rewarded. If you don't make your numbers, you get no bonus. The larger the company, the larger the budget, and the greater responsibility you'll have to meet your goals. Salaries are fairly comparable across the board—working at a larger or more prestigious company doesn't necessarily translate to more money.

Show me the money

Sales revenue minus the cost of goods sold yields the **gross profit.** If you sell an embroidered T-shirt for $7 and it only cost you $4 to make, your gross margin equals $3. If you have to mark down the shirt to $6, your gross profit will decrease. The gross profit divided by sales yields the **gross margin.**

Prospects

Securing an executive trainee position with a good store is the easiest way to start your career in buying. Competition for these training programs can be fierce, however, and with the closing and consolidation of so many large department stores there are actually fewer opportunities in buying now than there were a few years ago. (See page 137 for more information on executive trainee programs.) Executive training programs are important because without at least a year of previous experience under your belt or several internships, assistant buyer positions can be very hard to come by. At a store like Intermix, for example, the company may require you to spend one to three years as a sales associate on the store floor before they offer you a crack at being an assistant buyer. With two to three years of experience, you can advance from an assistant buyer position to an associate buyer. Usually, people spend two to three years as associate buyers before advancing to become buyers.

Job Titles

- **Merchandising Manager**

  These professionals manage teams of buyers to ensure that they follow the store's overall goals and financial plan. Merchandising managers generally oversee several related groups: For example, a manager might supervise the entire men's department, from tuxedos to sportswear to shoes. Or they might oversee the accessories department, making sure that all of the store's legwear, jewelry, and bags reflect a similar vision. If sequins are the hot new trend, the merchandising manager for accessories will see to it that everything sports a little bling.

- **Buyer**

  Buyers determine financial goals by forecasting, tracking sales of key items, and responding to sales and inventory for a specific area. They also develop the range of clothing sold in their store, balancing depth against breadth. The buyer strives to provide customers with everything they need and tries to expand that customer base by price point or demographic. Buyers work with vendors to secure the best deals and to ensure the timely delivery of goods, and they also develop advertising strategies and determine which items to feature in displays.

- **Associate Buyer**
  Associate buyers work with buying teams to develop sales strategies and define the assortment of fashions needed to meet those goals. They spend time in the stores, talking with customers and sales teams. They conduct and evaluate market tests to determine whether new items will sell. Associate buyers are expected to establish good relationships with vendors and participate in design direction meetings to provide input on the customer, price points, and sales trends. This is the stepping stone to eventually becoming a full buyer.

- **Assistant Buyer**
  Assistant buyers track assortment sheets and samples, purchase orders, make deliveries, and plan markdowns. They analyze competitors' pricing and research current trends. As an assistant buyer you'll study daily and monthly sales reports, recommending strategies to promote key items. You'll serve as a liaison between buyers and vendors, maintaining contracts and communicating changes in orders.

The Ground Floor

Most department stores have executive trainee programs for new buyers. In these programs, participants receive classroom training in a very structured program. They spend time "on the floor," checking out activity in the actual stores. They also assist the buyers, ensuring that shipments arrive on time and preparing spreadsheets to determine buying patterns. They may also tag along with their supervising buyer to market appointments, making recommendations on what to buy based on past sales. Executive trainees also get refresher courses in retail math and department store operations.

Being an assistant buyer is a lot like being an executive trainee, except without the classroom element. You will support the buyer every day in every way. You'll pull reports for your boss's research and meeting preparation. You'll complete basic tasks like process markdowns in the computer system so that sales prices ring up properly. And when the boss wants sales numbers, you're the person she will ask. During seasonal transitions—when one season is closing and another is starting—your arms and head will be filled with sales figures, markdown strategies, phone messages, and delivery schedules. Juggling, anyone?

PUBLIC RELATIONS

Public relations professionals are charged with capturing the public's attention—and then keeping it. PR folks manage a company's image, making sure that the brand name is on everyone's lips and people see the brand as desirable and attractive. They spend most of their time figuring out new, creative ways to get the product out in front of potential customers, which means they're constantly interacting with magazines and other media outlets. (Not to mention celebrities. Who do you think makes sure every young, trendy starlet is carrying the same handbag?) Many fashion companies have their own in-house PR departments, while others rely on outside PR firms or a combination of internal and external professionals. Especially in big fashion cities like New York and L.A., you can find entire PR firms that focus solely on fashion clients.

Personality Profile

If you love to write and are assertive and outgoing, this could be a great career path to explore. A bachelor's degree in marketing, journalism, English, or liberal arts is good preparation. Here are a few of the personality traits and skills that a public relations professional should have.

- **You love writing, and you love talking even more.** Excellent writing and speaking skills are absolutely essential in PR because your entire professional existence revolves around communication. You'll constantly be interacting with new people, trying to put your brand in the best light possible. You'll be wheedling magazine editors, schmoozing with trendsetters, and churning out press release after glittering press release. If you like to hole up with occasional fits of agoraphobia or are tentative with your words, this will not be the best place for you.

- **Oddly enough, "Network" is your middle name.** The ability to network is important in any business, but it's especially crucial in fashion PR. Public relations people have to have a wealth of contact information at their fingertips, and their ability to do their job well depends on their ability to build long-lasting, steady relationships with editors and other media folk. Extroverts will find this type of work very appealing.

- **Nothing gets you down.** If you work in public relations, you always have to be "on." That means being cheerful, professional, and prepared to deal with the stress of managing the million crises that can arise on a given day. You have to be able to manage your time effectively so that you can stay healthy, sane, and efficient. And keep in mind that you'll constantly be in the public eye, whether you're putting on huge parties and press conferences or tiny, exclusive functions—which means you better practice keeping a smile on your face for hours on end.

- **The latest gem of Page Six gossip? You saw it coming from a mile away.** Lucky you: A big part of being a good PR person is the ability to stay on top of pop culture. You need to be aware of the nuances of the celebrity landscape so you know who to focus your efforts on. If you're trying to get attention for your company's new glitzy, diamond-encrusted baguette handbag, you need to understand why Lindsay Lohan would be a better celeb placement than, say, Hillary Clinton.

- **You're a spin master who's always got an angle.** PR folks often have to take a great big nothing and turn it into something. Even if the fall collection was a total mess, with 30 completely random looks, it'll be your responsibility to craft a coherent story for the press that makes it all seem deliberate. "Oh that? That's the new urban jungle look. Chaos is totally in this season."

66 If you're in public relations, *Women's Wear Daily* is going to be your bible; it should be the first thing to hit your desk every morning. And your two most valuable tools are your Excel spreadsheet with all your industry contacts and your cell phone, where you can keep all your contacts' private phone numbers. I also highly recommend staying on top of the hottest new blogs. From Perez Hilton's gossip page to consumer websites, such as the Abercrombie blog, these are important sources of information on trends and buzz."

—Tom Handley, Public Relations/Marketing Specialist
Ralph Lauren, Badgley Mischka, Heidi Weisel, and Adrienne Landau

The Workplace

You'll most likely be based in an office, where you'll type away at press releases and brainstorm new events with your coworkers. That office will be littered with samples of your company's products, so they can be sent out to potential clients ASAP as needed. If *Marie Claire* is doing a story on animal prints, for example, you'd better be ready to messenger this season's leopard print hobo to their accessories editor at the drop of a tiger-striped hat. Your work will often take you off-site, as well. Your company might decide to stage a publicity event at the zoo, for example, to promote that new line of animal prints. (And you might be the one charged with convincing the PETA folks that it's all fake fur.)

This is a very social job, so be prepared to get your ear permanently soldered to your phone headset. You'll need to have a fat Rolodex at your fingertips, filled with contact info for caterers, security firms, and party rental services, not to mention editors at newspapers and magazines—with whom you're *always* on friendly terms, in the hopes that they'll give your products good press. But it's not all palm greasing and chitchatting: PR professionals have to be great project managers, since they constantly have to plan and coordinate complicated events. Excel will become your best friend. You need to be creative with set budgets—what do you do when you're given $75,000 to produce a runway show and $30,000 alone has to go to the Bryant Park tent rental?—and then manage the deployment of that budget. You'll also be the one dealing with all the nitty-gritty details, such as keeping guest lists updated and making sure that you've got the right number of chairs for a charity show.

Some PR companies give their employees a clothing allowance!

Prospects

Competition for entry-level positions in PR can be intense. The jobs are out there, but you have to be willing to swallow a low salary and mostly menial responsibilities at first. Those with a real passion who are willing to pay their dues, though, will move up in the ranks. Some assistants can move up within one to two years to become a PR coordinator or manager. The rate at which one advances, however, can vary widely with each individual firm. Ultimately, in PR you're always the sum of your Rolodex. Getting promoted and landing new clients requires phenomenal connections on top of your already stellar communication skills.

After working for a year or two at an agency, many PR professionals segue into working in-house for a particular brand, where the pay is often better. Agency jobs will expose you to a wide range of clients and products—making it a great first stop for entry-level employees—but when you work in-house you'll absorb the culture of a single brand.

There's also a lot of work available for freelance PR professionals, which can be a great way to get your foot in the door at a big agency. Plenty of fashion companies don't have the budget to continuously retain the services of a big PR firm but are willing to pay a freelancer quite well for helping extend their brand into new markets ($3,000 a month is a typical rate for full-time freelance PR services). You might start by checking out the listings on Craigslist for marketing, PR, and advertising gigs: New York–based firms and those based elsewhere advertise there. A Salt Lake City store, for example, might need a freelance PR person in New York to keep in touch with New York magazine editors and messenger over samples when necessary. From there, you can start building up your network. PR specialists find most of their clients through word of mouth, so you need to be your own best publicist and stay in the loop.

Salaries

An entry-level public relations job can pay as little as $25,000 to $35,000 per year. But don't panic! With some experience you will be able to make $40,000 to $60,000 as a PR executive. A director of public relations can earn $80,000 to well over $100,000. And if you manage to grab the brass vice presidential ring, your income level will far exceed $100,000.

Job Titles

- **VP of Public Relations**

  With over 10 years of experience, these professionals work with top execs, from Saks to Zac Posen, to build a direction for the brand and strengthen the brand's integrity. They help coordinate the direction of the current season as well as long-term planning for the line.

- **Director of Public Relations**

  The director supervises the entire public relations department. A more managerial position, the director of PR spot generally requires seven years of experience or more.

- **Public Relations Executive**

  With three to five years' experience, a public relations assistant can move up and become a PR exec. This job entails activities such as writing press releases, arranging news conferences, and setting up media interviews with designers or company executives.

- **Public Relations Assistant**

  PR assistants spend their time writing (and rewriting!) press releases, maintaining databases of client information, developing new ways of networking, sending out product samples to magazines and other media outlets, and coordinating various event details.

The Ground Floor

As a public relations assistant, your job entails supporting your supervising PR executive in developing media outreach strategies—plus anything else that needs to be done, from answering his calls to setting up his lunch appointments. You'll operate as your boss's sponge and seeker of information, funneling all the hot details you find about the market, celebs, or the media to your supervisor, who will then organize and implement promotional strategies.

All PR specialists work with the media to ensure that writers, editors, and tastemakers have access to their client's latest products. You'll also research and coordinate wardrobe opportunities for movies, television programs, and celebrity appearances. Working closely with wardrobe stylists is an essential part of the job. When it comes time to get the hottest bag or that must-have distressed, embellished T-shirt in the public eye, stylists will become your best friends, since they provide a direct conduit to celebrities and their oh-so-desirable product placement. Want Katie Couric to sport your new platinum hoops on the *CBS Evening News*? Better get chummy with the show's wardrobe coordinator. In addition to the media, public relations pros work closely with retailers (Bergdorf Goodman, Neiman Marcus, or Saks Fifth Avenue, for example) to get the word out about their clients and products.

A typical day for a PR assistant might involve coordinating loan-outs of garments and accessories to celebrities for a red carpet appearance or to magazines for photo shoots, writing press releases, and pitching story ideas to feature writers at magazines and other news media, such as popular websites and blogs. Another typical assistant task is summarizing all editorial coverage for the brand from the past month: recapping all media mentions, compiling the advertising costs and estimated number of customers reached, and copying all credits for the photos of the company's products that appeared in print or online.

THE CAREER GENIE

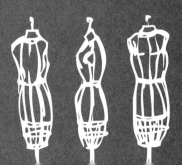

The Career Genie looks into his crystal ball to predict the career fortunes of six eager job seekers. What does the future hold for you? Compare yourself to these brave young souls.

~~~~~~~~~~~~~~~~~~~~~~~~~~~~~~~~~~

Elizabeth

SNAPSHOT

Elizabeth, 22, has her finger firmly on the pulse. Whenever she's out, scenesters beg her to tell them where she shops. And shop she does—although her passion for "it" bags, combined with her hefty student loan debt, seems to concern her parents more than her.

Elizabeth just graduated from Pratt Art Institute with a BFA in fashion design and has done several internships at prominent design houses, including Narciso Rodriguez and Calvin Klein. At both companies, she proved her incomparable work ethic by staying late, getting in early, and pitching in when deadlines started creeping up. Now that she's on the market for a full-time job, Elizabeth is trying to figure out whether she wants to work for a designer collection at a small house or a mass-market sportswear line at a larger company.

OUTLOOK

Elizabeth has really positioned herself well for an entry-level assistant designer job. She has an undergrad degree in design, so she's sure to bring the requisite technical and artistic skills to the table. With two internships under her belt, Elizabeth is ready for the long hours, hard work, and staff hierarchy. Elizabeth needs to reach out to her network now to connect with job opportunities. She should also participate in Pratt's student runway show—a nice perk that comes with attending an industry-leading institution.

Elizabeth needs to be aware that an entry-level salary in New York City will just barely cover her rent and student loan payments, so she'll need to buckle down with a budget.

Patti

SNAPSHOT

Patti, 25, got her BA at Ohio University, where she majored in math and computer science. She's meticulous and detail-oriented and has always had a way with words as well as numbers. Her only real job experience was at a high-end fragrance boutique, but she was the top salesperson there two summers running.

Patti's mom taught her to use a sewing machine when she was young, and since then she's always sewn a few pieces a year. Though she isn't the type who has to be the center of attention, she's crazy about fashion and wants a piece of it. Her family wanted her to have a traditional college experience, so she attended a liberal arts school instead of getting a design degree. She's now considering going back to school for a fashion design degree, but she's still paying back student loans and is wary of taking on more debt.

OUTLOOK

Initially, Patti's biggest hurdle is that her passion for fashion is greater than her hands-on experience. She needs to get intensive training in design, preferably at a well-known fashion or art school, before she'll be seriously considered for assistant designer jobs. It's going to be a long slog, but Patti needs to be realistic—competition for these coveted entry-level jobs can be fierce, and she'll be up against applicants with four years of training under their belts, not to mention excellent faculty contacts.

It takes a lot of time to master design skills, and the cost of living and studying in a major fashion center could send her debt skyrocketing. She may have to consider working full-time and taking classes at night. Patti should realize, though, that great job opportunities exist in her own backyard: Abercrombie & Fitch has design headquarters in Columbus, Ohio.

If Patti can't find an assistant designer position but is still dying for a place in the fashion universe, she should consider working as a technical designer, which will utilize her fastidious nature as well as her math and computer background. Patti's comfort with playing a supporting role and her excellent people skills will make her a great fit for this job.

Natasha

SNAPSHOT

Natasha, 28, has just finished a yearlong associate's degree in fashion studies at FIT. Since her undergraduate days at UMich, where she majored in English, Natasha has had to work hard to overcome a learning disability, which keeps her from processing verbal information as well as she does written material.

Natasha has a very classic, feminine style—think Jackie O meets Charlotte York—which she parlayed into a retail job at the like-minded kate spade last semester. Her favorite part of the job was helping her boss assemble the window displays, since she used to design sets and costumes for the college opera society.

Natasha has always thought well in three dimensions, has excellent drawing skills, and, for someone with fairly traditional tastes, Natasha loves the unexpected—for one of her final accessory design projects, she turned a pair of mother-of-pearl doorknobs into a fabulous pair of shoulder-dusting earrings.

OUTLOOK

Accessory design is a wide-open field, with plenty of opportunities to create everything from handbags to belts to shoes. Natasha's background makes her a good candidate for this field. Natasha also has a great undergraduate education with an emphasis on literature and writing—that'll be a big bonus to employers who expect her to have excellent communication skills. She'll have to keep working hard to compensate for her learning disability, though.

Natasha will also have to build a really sharp, professional-looking portfolio. She might consider spending a summer in an accessory design internship, where she can sketch, source fabric and trims, and get feedback on putting together her portfolio. If Natasha doesn't want to stay in New York, positions in accessory design can be found all over the country. Natasha might also want to consider visual merchandising, which would draw on both her exquisite taste and her talent for spatial thinking.

Hiroshi

SNAPSHOT

Growing up in fashion-forward Tokyo, Hiroshi, 23, developed fantastic style. His closet is stacked to the rafters with limited-edition sneakers and T-shirts, but he also knows how to scour thrift stores to unearth unexpected gems.

Hiroshi moved to California with his family six years ago. Since English is his second language, he's worked hard to improve his communication skills. His determination landed him a spot at UC Berkeley, where he got his BA in history and theater.

Hiroshi is endlessly curious about the world and devours information on everything from pop culture to international politics. He had a variety of part-time gigs during college: everything from spinning on his college radio station to costuming the summer opera. Ever since he saw Philip Bloch cover the Oscars, he's been dreaming of becoming a stylist.

OUTLOOK

Hiroshi has the number-one trait for being a great stylist: major style. Hiroshi's full-scale immersion in popular culture—everything from fashion to theater to opera to the fine arts—makes him a natural for this line of work.

Hiroshi should realize that there are very limited opportunities for stylists, and assignments are almost entirely freelance. The best way to break in is to work with an established pro, so Hiroshi should make a list of stylists whose work he loves and contact their agents about the possibility of assisting. He should also look into gigs at fashion magazines, even part-time or as an intern, to gain insight into editorial work. If he feels that he needs a steady paycheck, a job in the market editorial or art departments of a fashion magazine might be far more attractive (although just as difficult to land).

One of Hiroshi's primary challenges will be proving that he's mastered English. He should continue to work on his language skills, investing in some continuing education classes if necessary. Hiroshi should also keep in mind that most stylist work is in New York or L.A.; since he's already familiar with California, L.A. might be an easier transition.

Krysta

SNAPSHOT

Krysta, 21, is just about to graduate from the University of Oregon with her bachelor's in business administration. She's always been a whiz with numbers, and in college she aced all her merchandising math classes. She's highly self-confident and loves being in charge, having organized events for her sorority and led groups during freshman orientation her senior year. She's a multitasker extraordinaire who knows how to handle lots of tasks without losing her cool.

Krysta comes from a long line of athletes. She played on her university softball team all four years and did a merchandising internship with Nike last summer. She's not your typical jock, though—she loves shopping and would love to find a way to combine her love of fashion with her business acumen.

OUTLOOK

Krysta's already well positioned to pursue an assistant merchandiser position. A degree in business shows that she can crunch numbers with the best of them. Her excellent people skills will come in handy, as merchandisers spend a lot of their time liaising between various departments.

The good news is that the job market is fairly healthy, since many large retailers are spinning off new stores (such as Gap's new Forth & Towne venture or Abercrombie's Ruehl and Hollister lines). Each new offshoot means more opportunities. Merchandising jobs exist in lots of major cities, so Krysta doesn't necessarily have to move to New York or Los Angeles. Some great fashion companies call Oregon home, including Adidas and her former employer Nike, so she should check with the U of O career center in addition to reaching out to her former supervisor at Nike.

Activewear companies will find her athletic experience particularly attractive, so Krysta should definitely emphasize her time on the softball team when applying to those companies. Without any experience in the fashion industry beyond her internship, Krysta will really need to sell her "soft" skills—her enthusiasm and social skills—along with her business expertise.

Rod

SNAPSHOT

Rod, 26, is a mover and a shaker. Famous for throwing the best parties in town—everything from glittery fundraisers to elegant at-home dinner soirees—Rod has never been afraid to strike up a conversation with a total stranger. Rod has a reputation for being a go-to guy, and friends and associates always turn to him in a crisis.

Rod is a third-generation graduate of the University of Missouri, married to his college sweetheart. He was an English major and excelled in his studies, in part because he's super disciplined and hyper-organized. Since graduating, he's worked as a features writer for *Experience Kansas City* magazine, where he covers arts and leisure and writes the occasional piece on Kansas City history. Rod's been interested in fashion PR ever since he helped organize a charity fashion show for the Children's Mercy Hospital.

OUTLOOK

Rod has the right kind of personality and background for a career in PR. His extensive writing experience will enable him to pen and edit press releases with ease, and his detail-oriented nature will help him handle the responsibilities of organizing events and coordinating media initiatives.

Rod will have to accept that Kansas City is not New York, though. It's a large enough city to find good PR jobs, but it'll be hard to find one that focuses on the fashion industry. An interim step might be to cover fashion for one of the regional magazines in Kansas City. He could also look into marketing-related opportunities with fashion companies, department stores, and local magazines.

Eventually, if Rod wants to hit the big time, he'll have to move to New York or Los Angeles. Even though he's a bit older than most interns, he should consider spending a summer at a fashion PR company; it could be the foot in the door that he needs to land a full-time gig. Since Rod's whole family is in Missouri—and he has a wife in the equation—he may need to consider options closer to home.

PART II: HOW TO BREAK IN

3

PREPARING YOURSELF FOR THE JOB SEARCH

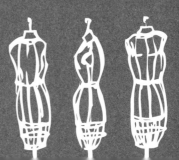

No one's going to give you a job just because you're good-looking and you ask nicely. Before heading out into the job market, you need to take a good, long look at your abilities and experiences. As you read the following lists, compare them to yourself. What are the areas in which you're lacking? Think about how you can beef up those areas, either with further training or volunteering. What are the things you *know* you're good at? Consider how you can prove and demonstrate those abilities to potential employers. Then, once you've assessed yourself as a candidate, it's time to market yourself in one pretty package—the all-important résumé.

IDENTIFY KEY DESIGN SKILLS

Design jobs require a much more extensive, specific set of skills than other fields in the fashion industry, such as public relations and buying. This is even true at the entry level: Beginning designers really have to hit the ground running. You'll obviously be honing your craft once you're hired, but truly competitive candidates have the following skills and characteristics under their belts from the get-go.

- **A well-defined aesthetic:** Strong design candidates have a distinct point of view that they can clearly articulate. "Um, I like to make pretty things?" just won't cut it. Being able to define your **aesthetic** and your **taste level** will help brand you as a candidate and allow potential employers to determine whether you belong with their company. Make a list of designers whose work has influenced you. Read descriptions of their collections; does any of it apply to you? Practice describing your work to friends. That way, in an interview, you can casually toss off something like, "I'd say my work is pretty cerebral, along the lines of Viktor & Rolf, but with a definite street edge inspired by Japanese youth subcultures." Defining your aesthetic will also help you focus your job search, since you'll be able to target companies that you can relate to and whose products you can feel passionate about.

66 The most successful designers have a distinct point of view that they remain true to. That aesthetic speaks for you, it's what you represent— essentially, it's your voice. It's important to find your point of view and maintain it, yet you must respond and adapt to the spirit of the times without compromising your signature."

—**Carmela Spinelli,** Associate Chair
Department of Fashion Design, Parsons

- **An ability to generate ideas:** Designers often have to produce multiple takes on a single project, and when some of those concepts don't work out or get shot down, they have to jump right up with even more. You can demonstrate this ability with a well-stocked **croquis** book, with drawings of multiple solutions to various projects. These sketches can show a potential employer your thought process and problem-solving skills.

- **Trendspotting skills:** As a designer, you need to stay on top of hot trends and incorporate them into your work. Your eyes should always be open, and you should pay attention to what everyone—everyone— is wearing. You'll need to articulate your influences for potential employers, so make sure you can talk easily about what excites your eye and your mind. Make it a point to mention those inspirations in your cover letter. In an interview, bring mood boards and sketches that reflect your trend-spotting ability. Finally, the clothes you wear to the interview should reflect your ability to put together a stylish, on-trend outfit appropriate for a business setting.

- **Historical knowledge:** Don't worry: Employers aren't going to ask you questions about the Napoleonic wars or medieval mercantile activity along the Silk Road. But knowledge of fashion history— especially in the category you want to work in—will make you a better designer. If you've taken any classes on fashion history, make sure to list them on your résumé.

- **Experience working on a team:** The fashion industry works on tight timelines and requires team players with flexibility, patience, and a "can do" attitude. Increasingly, employers are asking candidates for evidence of team experience. Volunteering as a dresser is a great way to demonstrate your ability to take direction and work collaboratively. Did you ever sit on a planning committee for a big school event, like a dance or a fashion show? Work in a community volunteer program? Those are all experiences you can highlight on your résumé.

- **Communication abilities:** The ability to explain yourself clearly, both through your sketches and during oral presentations (**pitches**) is huge. You also need the ability to take direction and correction without drama or defensiveness. And remember: Being a good communicator doesn't mean talking all the time, so don't feel the need to blast your interviewer with a mile-a-minute verbal tirade. Having a really strong, well-designed résumé and a well-written cover letter can go a long way toward proving that you know how to present yourself well and get your point across effectively. So don't even think about skimping on them.

Some good starter projects are raglan-sleeved blouses, kimonos, or even simple pillowcases.

- **Basic construction and sewing knowledge:** Knowing how a garment is actually sewn is key to a designer's success, even if you're not planning on becoming a technical designer. You should have some experience constructing garments so that when the time comes to develop concepts you know how design things that can actually be manufactured. Even if you've never enrolled in a sewing class, you can learn a lot by doing. Get yourself a sewing machine, a pattern, and the necessary fabric and notions and give it a shot!

- **Drawing proficiency:** Sketching and illustration are essential drawing skills that any assistant designer must possess. In many entry-level jobs you'll be expected to execute excellent **flat sketches.** If you are unsure about the level of your drawing skills, try to get feedback from faculty or other students or possibly even your internship supervisor. If you're not in school, compare your sketches against those in the textbook *Fashion Illustration* by Kathryn Hagen.

- **Familiarity with draping techniques:** The design process involves fitting fabric to a mannequin, or **draping.** Designers carefully pin the fabric to make sure that it lies flat, covers the right places, and, of course, looks good. The draped garment is the basis for making the patterns for that garment. If you are serious about studying fashion design, think about buying a mannequin to practice on. (Hello, eBay!)

- **Experience with fabric and trim development:** Assistant designers typically do a lot of the necessary "shopping" in the raw materials markets, searching out fabrics and trims. Your knowledge of textiles and their characteristics, along with a practical understanding of how to use them effectively, will put you ahead of the game.

- **Computer skills:** Entering the job market as an assistant designer requires good computer skills. Adobe PhotoShop and Illustrator are used heavily to make color corrections, flat sketches, and mood boards. Microsoft Excel is used to create cost sheets and track samples. Local colleges often offer weekend or evening courses in these programs, and for the more tech savvy, basic programs like Excel can be learned with the help of books or training software. Most people will need to take classes in PhotoShop and Illustrator, however, to reach an acceptable skill level.

- **Understanding of color theory:** As an entry-level designer, you need to have a good eye for color so that you can tell whether samples from the dye house match the original color swatch provided by the design team. You can't settle for lipstick red when your boss specifically asked for carnelian! You also need to know how colors work together. When your design team decides that this season will be all about pinks and purples—a pairing whose logic is clear to you— you need to be able to identify complementary colors and neutrals to create a coherent collection.

IDENTIFY KEY PRODUCTION SKILLS

Working in production is all about being a consensus builder. It's your job to help various team members come to agreement on everything from fabrics to delivery schedules. Employers are looking for people who can take on leadership roles but don't need to be the ultimate authority or the constant center of attention: Drama queens need not apply, but efficient stage managers are always welcome. To have a successful career in production, you'll also need the following skills.

- **A facility with retail math and a laserlike attention for details:** Production people balance the merchandisers' requests and the designers' needs against the reality of the manufacturing process, which often comes down to pricing issues. You need to understand how the cost of producing a garment relates to sales price and how those numbers work out on a mass scale. You'll often use computer programs to process these figures, but employers will want to know that you could crunch those numbers yourself with a calculator and some scratch paper, if it came down to that. Attention to detail is obviously important when dealing with financial matters, but you'll also be keeping spreadsheets with details relating the production process and monitoring calendars for the various departments, so you always need to keep your eyes on the ball.

- **Experience in a relevant market:** Different markets have different production requirements—womenswear companies, for example, generate a much greater range of products on a much faster timeline than menswear companies, which tend to stress quality, fit, and consistency over innovation. Makers of children's clothing, in turn, have to worry about safety issues such as flammable material and cords, fasteners, or trims that might pose a choking hazard. As in any industry, it's easy to get pigeonholed, so if you want to keep your options open, try to intern at a company that produces various lines in different markets. Also remember that it's generally easier to transition from the high end to the lower end of the industry.

- **A knack for smooth negotiations:** Production people have to deal with a wide variety of professionals every day, all of whom want very specific things. You'll have to be the bad guy in a lot of conversations—the one who tells the designers that they can't afford 10,000 bags' worth of that jade striped cloth from Italy, but that they can afford a similar fabric manufactured in China. You'll also be negotiating with vendors and factories, many of which may be located overseas, and you need to do it all with a smile on your face. Highlighting your interpersonal skills and any team-building experience on your résumé will make you an attractive candidate.

- **An ability to bring projects to the finish line:** Production is like the legman in a relay race: You're the one who's responsible for bringing it all home. You need to keep everyone on schedule and make sure everything gets turned around in a timely fashion. After all, if items are late in the stores, managers won't be calling the designers, merchandisers, or account execs—they'll be calling you. Production people need to be assertive enough to spur other departments when necessary while also being conscious of their own deadlines. If you're indecisive and need lots of time to mull over decisions, you're not going to be effective in this department.

66 Clothing is like produce—it comes with an expiration date. No one wants to buy two-day-old bread and no one wants to buy outdated fashions. It's production's job to make sure those clothes get out there while they're still fresh."

—**Barbara Knapp,** Head of Production
Rogan LLC

- **Foresight:** "A stitch in time saves nine" is the production person's motto. You need to be able to anticipate problems long before they arise, which means you need to understand the entire process from start to finish and get involved long before the garments are ready to be manufactured. It's your job to provide a reality check for the other team members, such as designers who want to use a process that's too costly or time-intensive. Any experience you have planning and overseeing long-range projects is important to emphasize on your résumé.

IDENTIFY KEY PR SKILLS

Public relations is all about creating "buzz" for your products, whether that buzz gets generated on the runway or as the result of sponsoring a skateboard park. The good news is that applicants for PR jobs don't have to tackle the mountain of requirements that their design brethren do. But wait! That doesn't mean you can just waltz into a company and pick up a job whenever you feel like it. You still need to brand yourself carefully and package yourself with flair. Savvy job hunters will emphasize the following in their résumés and applications.

- **Writing ability:** To be a good PR person, you need be able to write clearly, efficiently, and articulately. If you have any journalism, grant writing, or technical writing experience, make sure to mention it. A class in public relations writing or copy editing is the perfect way to beef up your skills.

- **Public speaking experience:** No hiding behind desks for these hardworking folks: PR people have to be comfortable speaking up. If you've led any student groups in school, you probably have quite a bit of public speaking experience. If you get queasy when you have to get up in front of people, take a class in public speaking or consider joining Toastmasters, an international organization whose members work on developing effective communication and leadership skills (toastmasters.org).

- **Persuasiveness:** A good PR person is a good salesperson and a charming negotiator. A big part of your job will be getting the press to cover your product. If *ELLE* is doing a piece on technology-influenced footwear, you better be able to convince the editor to showcase your company's new line of stilettos made from computer chips. You need to be able to pitch ideas in a compelling way, which often involves attaching your product to a big-name celebrity. ("Come on, Mr. Editor, Sienna's been snapped at Starbucks three times with our new leather duffle on her arm!") Any sales experience should definitely be highlighted on your résumé.

- **Diplomatic acumen:** On the business side of this industry, like in any other industry, things can go wrong. But when they go wrong at a major trade show, you need to think on your feet, solve problems, and have everyone feeling good about your solutions. You've got to be tough to turn people away from a private fashion show, especially when those people are celebrities. PR mavens know how to be firm yet tactful. Leadership roles in school clubs or organizations are good to emphasize, as well as any experience you may have had working with high-profile personalities.

- **Knowledge of the industry:** To work on the business end of fashion you need to be fully aware of all the major fashion companies, with a firm grasp on who the big players are, who's buying out whom, which hot young designer is switching houses, and anything else related to the money side of the industry. In an interview you should be able to reference *WWD* articles related to the recent acquisitions and current activities of the fashion house (or the clients of the PR firm) you're interviewing with.

- **Trend awareness:** PR folks make it their business to know what's hot. Spend time in all kinds of stores, from boutiques to department stores to mass merchants. See what people are buying, what they're wearing, and what combination of bags they're carrying (so you can learn about customer shopping patterns). On your résumé, you can list "trend forecasting" under skills, in addition to noting significant travel to places such as Europe or Japan that could inform your awareness of upcoming trends.

66 I constantly have to be aware of what's happening around me, both at work and on the street. I need to know everything from who's on what cover of which magazine all the way down to what restaurants are opening that week. Fashion is so fickle, and it's my job to make sure our brand always seems like we know things first."

—**Dan Strassburger,** Marketing Coordinator
Donna Karan

- **Retail experience:** If you've had any sales experience in fashion, make the most of it. You've undoubtedly listened to customers, solved problems, and folded your share of clothes. Except for the folding, these skills fit PR like a pair of vintage gloves. Public relations departments want to make connections with potential customers, so any previous retail experience will serve you well.

- **Event planning:** You need to be a master event planner who can keep cool while troubleshooting the myriad problems that inevitably crop up at the last minute. This could be anything from having to find an extra 100 chairs for a runway show starting in 10 minutes to suddenly realizing that Paris and Lindsay have been seated in the same row the day after a major tabloid war. And you need to pull it all off with flair and style. If you've ever organized a big dance or stage managed a play, you'll want to put that experience front and center on your résumé.

The Public Relations Student Society of America (prssa.org) offers members online courses, mentoring programs, and an annual conference full of networking opportunities.

- **An ability to see the big picture:** Whatever you do, you have to properly represent your company's overall brand vision. That goes for everything from the type of parties you throw to the magazines in which you place your products. Should Baby Phat advertise in Martha Stewart Living? Should you throw a big, glittery party after the MTV Movie Awards if your company makes eco-friendly hiking wear? It's all about strategic thinking. If you've ever raised money for a cause, such as breast-cancer awareness, or worked in sales and can describe in concrete terms how you improved the organization's ability to meet its goals, make sure to note this on your résumé or cover letter. In addition, read a broad range of fashion magazines, from *InStyle* to *Vogue* to

Seventeen, to see which companies get covered where. Look beyond the ads—since companies pay for that kind of placement, they're not as strong an indicator of what's hot as the fashion editorials. Also make sure to keep your eye on celebrity magazines like *People* and *Us Weekly*. If starlets keep showing up to red carpet events in Temperley dresses and Sigerson Morrison shoes, you can bet there's a great PR campaign behind it all.

IDENTIFY KEY MERCHANDISING, ACCOUNT SALES, AND BUYING SKILLS

These job titles relate to three different stages of a single business transaction: Merchandisers conceive and plan the product, account executives recommend product to the retail buyers, and then buyers purchase those products for sale in their stores. Jobs in these fields all require many of the same skills, from a facility with business math to smooth negotiating tactics.

- **A savvy eye for design:** Even if they're not the ones actually designing the clothes, buyers, merchandisers, and account executives all need to know how garments and accessories catch a consumer's interest, which requires discerning taste and the ability to analyze why something works—or doesn't. They also need to know how to create and combine products in fresh, exciting ways. Before your interview, think of stories you can share that illustrate your design skills, especially as they relate to business goals. For example, if you worked the sales floor at Saks Fifth Avenue and were put in charge of arranging the display of winter hats, make note of how you did this and what effect your work had on moving the product. If you did an incredible job of decorating the tables at a party or charity event, take pictures to show during your interview. Dressing stylishly or wearing a terrific accessory that you found at a flea market or picked up during your travels (even if you only went so far as the local crafts fair) is an easy way to highlight your keen sense of style.

- **Resourcefulness:** When buyers are at a showroom talking with the sales rep, they've got to keep a million things in mind, like how the merchandise fits in with what's already been purchased, how much floor space is available, and what colors are needed to make the selection of goods attractive to the customer. Merchandisers also have to deal with these kinds of creative puzzles on a daily basis, as they figure out how to apply one trend across several categories, and how to tailor those trends for their brand's particular style. If you've ever had to design something with certain constraints—say, a magazine or a theater set—or organize something on a budget and a deadline, you've definitely got a transferable skill that can be emphasized in your résumé or cover letter.

- **Trend awareness:** You probably already spend a lot of time poring over fashion magazines, so put all those subscriptions to use. Start collecting a clip file of trends and company news. Pay attention to the ways in which trends circulate, whether moving from the red carpet to the mall or from the street on up to the runway. You'll want to be able to talk intelligently about buying patterns in your interview, particularly if you're interviewing for merchandising or buying positions.

- **An outgoing, engaging personality:** Merchandisers need great interpersonal skills since they're charged with coordinating several manufacturing departments. Account execs need to establish a high level of trust and rapport with their buyers and get them excited about new product lines. And buyers need to be independent, outspoken individuals who are comfortable negotiating deals with vendors. In any of these fields, you'll constantly be collaborating and strategizing with others, so employers will look for indications that you've had a lot of experience working with others and taking on leadership roles. On your résumé, emphasize any clubs and organizations you may have led as well as any customer service positions you held.

- **An ability to think quickly and behave calmly under pressure:** Fashion is a fast-paced industry: You only have so much time to capitalize on a trend before it evaporates. Buying, merchandising, and working as an account exec are all very time-sensitive fields, so to be successful you must be able to work independently and make decisions on the fly. Highlight any experience that required you to work under pressure—say, stage managing a play or coordinating a charity run.

- **Fluency in foreign languages:** If you speak another language, you may be able to communicate with factories, suppliers, or buyers in other parts of the world. If you're working with companies in Europe, French and Italian are helpful. Many companies have manufacturing facilities in Latin America or in Asia, so Spanish, Korean, Vietnamese, or any of several Chinese dialects could be to your advantage. At the same time, your ability to write and read in English is critical.

66 Buying is not glitz and glam. It is not runways and celeb-studded parties. Buying is MATH. Historical data manages a buy, not whimsy or feelings."

—**Adam Reiter,** CEO
Thefashiontool.com

- **A facility with retail math:** Take an honest look at your skills here. On the business end of the industry, you'll spend a fair amount of time reading and analyzing reports, so you have to be on friendly terms with numbers. You'll need to calculate gross margins, markdowns, and sales in order to manage your business. If you have a background in finance or economics, make sure to emphasize that experience in your résumé. If you've never taken a retail math course, you should look into taking some classes.

- **Recordkeeping and organizational skills:** As a buyer, you'll need to remember what you ordered, in what sizes and colors, from whom, for what ship date, and the names of the sales rep's kids (just for good measure). Account execs need to track, by department, who's taking what markdown and when and ensuring that everyone meets their order plans. Merchandisers need to make line plans and track samples so they know how many pieces have gone out to editors, PR reps, and department stores. Unless you have a bionic memory, you'll never be able to keep all this info in your head, so you'll need to know how to use spreadsheet software or a computerized inventory tracking system. Employers will want to see someone they can trust with large amounts of data, so make sure to highlight any times when you had to manage complicated plans or spreadsheets. When you show up for an interview, make sure your bag is neat (no papers and water bottles spilling out when you unzip it) and your clothes tidy and well-pressed: You'll come across as trustworthy and organized.

- **Sales experience:** As a merchandiser, account exec, or buyer, your eyes are on one prize: the consumer. After all, your goal is to create, sell, and select fashions that people will purchase in enough quantities so that your company turns a tidy profit. Any retail experience you've had will be useful, as it'll give you insight into consumer buying patterns. If your sales experience dovetails nicely with the brand identity of the company you're interviewing with, play it up. If you spent three semesters working at a hip boutique that was known for having the hottest jeans on the block, Diesel will want to know about it.

- **Market awareness:** It's not enough to know about the company you're interviewing with: You also need to understand how that company fits into the bigger picture. If you're a merchandiser or account exec, you need to know who else is fighting for dominance in the same market share so you can stay updated on developments that might affect your bottom line. As a buyer, you need to understand the range of vendors you buy garments and accessories from, as well as the other stores your customers visit.

CRAFT A KILLER RÉSUMÉ

Your résumé gets you in the door. Employers can get literally hundreds of résumés every week, so it's important that yours stand out from the pack. Designers often think that their work should speak for itself and that a résumé seems unimportant. But the reality is that the company gatekeeper is often a human resources person who will gauge your value as a candidate purely on the strength of your résumé. Instead of thinking of it as a chore, think of your résumé as an opportunity to define and brand yourself as a highly desirable employee. Here are 10 basic tips on how to make a résumé that will get you noticed.

1. **Figure out what to emphasize.** Put yourself in the employer's shoes and think about what they want from you. Use the sections above as a guideline. Even if you're applying as a designer, employers will want to see that you've had some real-life work experience so they won't have to worry about training you to do simple tasks. Put your emphasis on three things: education, work experience, and skills.

2. **Limit it to one page.** Consider this a mandatory rule. HR folks want to quickly scan and digest the crucial information on your résumé. They're not interested in the details at this point: That's what the interview is for. Ruthlessly edit your text and only include what's essential. Keep it brief and to the point, and make sure that each responsibility listed for a particular job takes up no more than one or two lines of text. Avoid long paragraphs or large blocks of text.

3. **Consider aesthetics.** Your résumé should be easy to read and understand within a 5- to 10-second scan. Believe it or not, most employers only give a résumé a few seconds of their attention before they decide to toss it or contact the candidate—they often get so many résumés that they can't spend 10 minutes reviewing every résumé. Your special qualities and essential work experience need to be easy to see at a glance. Use an appealing layout that guides the reader's eye to the most crucial information. A jam-packed, complicated résumé printed in a tiny typeface in order to adhere to the one-page rule will go straight in the garbage. Keep your résumé as simple as possible. Use a font large enough to decipher at a single glance (11- or 12-point) and use standard $8\frac{1}{2}$ x 11 inch paper. Don't be tempted to use brightly colored paper or wacky fonts just to draw attention to your résumé. If you want it to stand out while remaining professional and elegant, find a design student at your school or local college and ask them to help you out.

4. **Organize your experience.** When putting together a résumé, you should organize your experience chronologically. List your education and employment in order, with the most recent experience at the top of the page. Make sure to keep your résumé totally up to date, noting any recent fashion-related experience, even if it's freelance or part-time.

5. **Energize your résumé.** When describing your past job responsibilities, use action verbs such as *expanded, created, managed, designed,* and *coordinated.* Rather than "Did cash register receipts," write, "Managed cash transactions," to make it more active and impressive. Also, if you're feeling stumped for work experience that seems related to fashion or that's really related to the particular job, think about transferable skills you may have from past art education classes or service jobs such as painting, writing, and customer service experience.

6. **Ruthlessly eliminate typos.** Don't underestimate the power of the typo. An errant period, a misspelled word, or a misplaced modifier is all an HR person needs to chuck your résumé. If you can't represent your best self now, at the point when it's entirely critical to make a good impression, how would you represent the company as an employee? Don't rely on spell-check to catch all your mistakes. Read it carefully, read it again, and then get someone else to read it. If you've got any friends with publishing experience, trade them a beer for a copyedit.

7. **Make it professional.** Use an easy, modest email address. "Iamterrific@wonderfulme.com" or "diva#1@hottmail.com" are not the most professional-sounding addresses. Create a real, honest-to-God grownup email address for yourself, preferably incorporating your last name.

8. **Don't get too personal.** Don't include your birth date, photo, or hobbies that an employer doesn't need to know about. The employer doesn't really need to know that you practice tae kwon do if he's looking to hire someone who can design a hot wrap dress or plan a great spring launch. If you're applying at The North Face, however, make sure to mention your summers spent backpacking the John Muir Trail.

9. **Seek wise counsel.** Who do you know in the fashion industry who could look at your résumé? Does your high school or college career counselor know about this industry? (Many, unfortunately, do not.) If that's the case, try making an appointment with the admissions office at an art school to find out about career options. What resources does your career center have? Ask for books on careers in fashion, get a password to the college's online job board, and find out if your school's career center has a reciprocity agreement with an art school that might share resources. You can also check out the National Portfolio Day Association, which hosts events around the country in which major art schools talk with high school students (npda.org). If you go, ask questions about what fashion employers look for in a résumé or ideal candidate.

10. **Do a real-world check.** Buy three weeks' worth of *Women's Wear Daily* and make a list of the requirements that employers are asking for in your field. Compare your résumé to the list. If you checked most of the requirements, chances are you'd be a competitive candidate.

SAMPLE RÉSUMÉS

Now that you've mastered these tips, we're going to show you the résumés of four job-seekers looking for entry-level jobs in fashion. Each applicant comes to the table with a different background, but they all follow the 10 steps to a T, creating clear, well-designed résumés that market themselves as compellingly as possible. Read their résumés and our commentaries, then get inspired to write your own!

SAMPLE DESIGN RÉSUMÉ

Susan Lee

4241 Lemon Avenue
Los Angeles, CA 90042
(213) 555-2118
SusanLee42@geemail.com

Objective	Seeking an assistant design position in women's apparel
Education 2007	*Rhode Island School of Design,* Providence, RI Bachelor of Fine Arts in Fashion Design
Skills	Proficient in Illustrator, Photoshop, Excel, QuarkXpress, U4ia Excellent skills in flat sketching, patternmaking, and construction

Work Experience

July 2007–present **Target Corporation,** Minneapolis, MN
CFDA Postgraduate Intern, Softlines

- Work with Kids', Men's, Women's, and Intimates design teams
- Develop and recolor prints for knits and wovens
  Digitally sketch flats
- Create directional boards and final design boards
- Manage library of fabric quality swatches from fabric expo

Summer 2006 **Gap Inc.,** New York, NY
Intern

- Participated in design process from concept to first sample,
  including trend research, shopping, and color forecasting
- Produced Illustrator-generated flats
- Utilized U4ia and did extensive illustration work
  for print design, repeats, and colorways

Spring 2005 **Gap Inc.,** Providence, RI
Sales Associate
Assisted customers, stocked shelves, organized merchandise

Honors 2006 Council of Fashion Designers of America, Scholarship
Dean's list all semesters, Parsons

References and portfolio available upon request

What's So Great About Susan's Résumé?

1. **She highlights her strengths.** Since Susan is just graduating from college, she makes sure to put the technical skills essential to entry-level jobs, such as flat sketching and computer skills, at the top and highlights the fact that she *does* have internship experience. Notice that she categorizes her competencies to show her wide range of skills and that she clearly marks her proficiency in the necessary software.

2. **She uses strong action verbs.** Susan's résumé contains over a dozen different verbs that describe the work she has done. Even though she's still in her first post-college job, she sells herself by choosing active, descriptive phrases such as *develop, create,* and *manage.*

3. **She clearly defines her experience.** Even though Susan's experience is mostly at the intern level, she makes the most of what she learned. She gives details about her internships, including research projects she worked on and specific duties she carried out, such as preparing information for overseas vendors.

4. **It's easy to read.** All subject headings are in bold, and the names of companies are in italics, making it easy to skim. She uses bullet points for added clarity.

5. **She showcases her accomplishments.** Showing your awards, including when you've made the dean's list or had other academic success, illustrates both your skills and your ability to apply yourself.

6. **She indicates that her references and portfolio are available upon request.** Employers usually don't need to contact your references until they're ready to interview you seriously, so it's not worth it take up valuable résumé real estate with their contact info.

Olivia Martinez

257 Rosetta Blvd. | Portland, OR 98765

555.576.3333 | omartinez07@martinez.com

EDUCATION

Portland State University, Portland, OR, 2007

Bachelor of Science, Marketing

EXPERIENCE

Adidas, Portland, OR, Sept. 2005–May 2007

Marketing Intern

- Studied sales trends for Adidas and competing companies
- Conducted surveys in urban and suburban malls
- Assisted with several promotional events, including sponsored sports events

McAllister Hall, Portland State University, Eugene, OR, Sept. 2005–May 2007

Resident Assistant

- Served as one of 12 live-in staff members for dormitory of 180 undergraduates
- Provided guidance, helped new students understand policies and procedures for residence halls and the college in general
- Participated as a team leader in staff meetings, retreats, social events, and floor events
- Responsible for six 12-hour shifts monthly as rotating night watch
- Trained in crisis management, team building, and conflict mediation

Center for Student Learning, Portland State University, Sept. 2003–Aug. 2005

Tutor

- Tutored in English and freshman math
- Provided in-person assistance and online composition review

Daisy's and Dolly's Florist, Eugene, OR, May 2002–Aug. 2003

Store Assistant

- Handled walk-in sales and kept inventory of materials on computer
- Assisted with set-up for major events (weddings, parties)

SKILLS

- Proficient in Microsoft Word, Excel, and PowerPoint; knowledge of QuickBooks; extensive experience with Internet research
- Experienced in event planning
- Excellent customer service skills and retail math background

What's So Great About Olivia's Résumé?

1. **She does a lot with a little.** Although Olivia is just graduating from college and has relatively little fashion-related experience, she makes sure to articulate the essential entry-level skills she possesses and highlights those skills by placing them in a special section at the top of the page. She also highlights the fact that she *does* have internship experience at an apparel company. And even though being a resident hall advisor may not seem immediately relevant, she clearly indicates the serious responsibilities she held, such as supervising others.

2. **She emphasizes transferable skills.** Olivia's only merchandising-related experience involved sales work at a florist's shop, but she highlights the fact that she *does* have transferable skills. Since experience working with people is so crucial in an entry-level merchandising job, for example, she details her experience as a resident assistant to illustrate that she has worked in such a context.

3. **She includes at least one big-name fashion brand in her work experience, and she makes it the first item in her experience record.** Getting an internship with Adidas was a smart move on Olivia's part. Whether you work the sales floor at the mall or complete an internship at corporate headquarters, getting a known fashion company on your résumé is an important part of branding yourself as a candidate. The Adidas internship links Olivia to a well-known, well-established company, indicating to other employers that she had the goods to land a competitive opportunity in the past. The experience with Adidas will be especially useful if Olivia wants to work with a company with a similarly active, urban aesthetic.

4. **She highlights skills in event planning and customer service.** These experiences would be valuable to any employer, but they're especially pertinent in merchandising. Event-planning experience shows that Olivia can juggle lots of details and manage communications, and customer service skills indicate that she understands consumer psychology.

SAMPLE PR RÉSUMÉ

Nathan Glick
89 1st Avenue
New York, NY 10078
glick@glick.com

Education:
University of Mississippi, Oxford, MS
Bachelor of Arts, English, May 2006

Experience:
National Public Radio
Public Relations Intern, Summer 2006, Washingon, DC
- Assisted the public relations team with assembling press kits
- Organized clippings for press archives
- Networked with local media, including magazines and television

University of Mississippi Student Newspaper
Contributing Writer, September 2004 to May 2006, Oxford, MS
- Gained journalism experience as regular reporter for school newspaper
- Edited work submitted by junior writers

Banana Republic
Cashier, September 2003 to May 2004, Oxford, MS
- Processed sales and handled returns
- Provided customer assistance
- Trained new employees as sales people

Awards:
$5,000 annual scholarship to University of Mississippi, 2002–2006

Extracurricular Activities:
- Debate team
- Student government

Skills:
- Microsoft Word, PowerPoint, Excel, experience with web design
- Excellent writing and public speaking skills

What's So Great About Nathan's Résumé?

1. **He clearly demonstrates a passion for words.** It's obvious that Nathan likes all forms of communication, which will serve him well in PR. He highlights the fact that he brings print and radio experience to the table, so he's already familiar with the various media outlets he'd be pitching stories to as part of a PR department.

2. **His career progression is evident.** Nathan started like a lot of college students—working retail. After that he progressed to working within his academic department at the school newspaper before landing an internship at a public radio station. Although he has no explicitly PR-related experience, his résumé doesn't have any holes, which can be red flags to potential employers.

3. **He keeps his information short and to the point.** Sometimes you don't need anything more than a short explanation. Don't try to pad your résumé with a lot of fluff that can't be backed up with concrete experience. Recruiters know how to look past that kind of inflation.

4. **He demonstrates that other people think he's worthy.** Nathan landed a great scholarship, evidence of his hard work and his ability to sell himself. List your most impressive awards on your résumé, even if they're not directly related to the job in question.

5. **He lists relevant extracurricular activities.** PR people need to communicate easily and effectively, so Nathan's debate and student government experience definitely makes for a nice résumé capper. Avoid the common mistake of listing activities that don't add to your candidacy. Employers don't really want to know that you like stamp collecting and long walks on the beach. But if you have a hobby that resonates with a company's aesthetic, definitely highlight it. For example, the board-sport company Volcom (with its mantra, "youth against establishment") loves to hire people who like music. And one recent intern at Warnaco managed to parlay her experience as a competitive high school swimmer into a gig designing Speedos for the Beijing Olympics. Always think about how you can tailor your résumé to speak more strongly to a particular employer. You never know when that extra step will make the difference.

SAMPLE BUYING RÉSUMÉ

Kevin Massey
84 Webster Groves Terrace
St. Louis, MO 65536
917-409-9877
massey4567@earthlinnk.com

Education
University of Missouri, Columbia, MO
Bachelor of Business Administration, May 2007
Study Abroad, Seoul Art and Design Institute, 2005–2006
Relevant Coursework: Statistics, Marketing, and International Business

Employment
The May Company, St. Louis, MO, June–August 2006
Intern, Corporate Retail
- Helped set up events when out-of-town buyers came to discuss strategies
- Handled administrative work, including filing and answering phones
- Processed weekly and monthly financial sales recaps

City of Columbia Parks and Recreation, Summers 2000–2005
Recreation Leader/Lifeguard
- Led team sports, including softball and basketball
- Taught Aikido
- American Red Cross–certified lifeguard

Thee and Me, Columbia, MO, January–August 2005
Salesperson
- Greeted customers and assisted them with purchases
- Handled cash transactions

Hobbies
Extensive travel in Southeast Asia

Skills
- Proficient in Illustrator, Photoshop, QuickBooks, Excel, MS Word, and PowerPoint
- Fluent in Korean

References
Attached

What's So Great About Kevin's Résumé?

1. **He demonstrates a history of continuous work experience.**
   Kevin accounts for every year since he graduated from high school;
   employers get very nervous when a résumé skips a summer (or a
   whole year).

2. **He makes his transferable skills evident.** Kevin makes it clear
   that he's well-versed in the kind of financial and administrative duties
   expected of an entry-level buyer. Kevin also knows how to work with
   people, having been a lifeguard for several years. Potential employers
   will know that, when the time comes for Kevin to start forming his
   own relationships with buyers, he'll already know how to deal calmly
   and professionally with new people.

3. **He shows a breadth of experience.** Kevin's résumé indicates that
   he can keep an eye out for people (lifeguard), can figure out complex
   problems (business degree), and has experienced other cultures (travel).
   He wisely used his last summer of college to get a fashion-related
   internship, which will make him a much more attractive candidate than
   other liberal arts grads.

4. **He presents his information concisely.** It can be tempting to fill
   up your résumé in order to look more experienced or impressive. Don't
   do it! A potential employer would much rather look at a clean, readable,
   brief document than one filled with stuff she has to read through.

5. **He has attached his references.** If you've given your references a
   heads-up and your current employer knows about your job search, then
   you can go ahead and add their contact info, especially if they're well-
   known or working in the field you wish to enter. However, if you want
   to keep your candidacy on the quiet, wait to be asked for your references.

ASSEMBLE YOUR PORTFOLIO

If you're applying for a job as a designer, you'll need a portfolio to accompany your résumé. As a design student and throughout your design career, your portfolio represents what you know how to do, what you've done, your aesthetic, your attention to detail, and your chosen direction. Recruiters, HR managers, and designers will be looking for two things: an aesthetic that matches the company's and demonstrated proficiency in conceptualization, sketching, colorways, trim selection, flat sketching, and, of course, creativity.

Pack a punch—but do it carefully

You can also use your portfolio to (carefully) demonstrate your sense of humor. One job applicant assembled a summer season portfolio with a nautical theme, in which every figure was drawn to look rather seasick. The illustrations could have been too much if they weren't backed up by excellent design concepts, and the student went on to receive several job offers. But a portfolio covered with pink faux fur might be pushing it, no matter what's inside. You can tell if your portfolio goes over the top by looking at people's faces when you present them with your book. If their mouths open and their eyebrows go way up, it's a good bet that you've gone too far. Words like *interesting, different,* or *unusual*—unless paired with words like *beautiful, fun,* or *excellent*—are clues that you've missed the mark.

---

10 Basic Elements of a Portfolio

Your portfolio is your sales pitch, all dressed up in black. A truly professional, well-balanced one will have all of the following.

1. **A quality cover:** Invest in a good, basic black portfolio, no bigger than 14 x 17 inches. The inside pages should be on ring binders or bound into the book, with acetate or clear plastic over black pages. Somewhere in the portfolio you should have a printed sticker or other label with your name and contact information. If you're unconventional, show it on the inside of your portfolio, not the outside. Save the leopard print for your bedroom.

2. **Four to six fashion groups:** These groups should each have a theme (for example, Romantic Victorian, Beach Party, or Winter Wedding) and show four to eight coordinated pieces. Don't show more than six groups or you'll overwhelm the reviewer. A good portfolio not only shows off your skills, ideas, and execution but also indicates that you know how to edit your work.

3. **A year's worth of seasons:** Your portfolio should span an entire year (spring, summer, fall, and winter/holiday) unless you are focusing on a very specific seasonal company, such as outerwear or swimwear.

4. **Flats and specs:** These showcase your ability to create technical sketches, either by hand or on the computer with Illustrator. Flats follow your fashion illustrations and often show both the front and back of each garment.

5. **Presentation board (mood board):** These boards display your inspirations for the collection that follows. They usually take the form of a collage of your research, photos, fabric or color swatches, and color theme, along with an image of the target customer.

6. **CAD work:** Increasingly, designers scan their sketches and use PhotoShop and Illustrator to change, color, and enhance the images. These digital images are often shared with design teams, production teams, and sales teams. Employers want to see examples of both your CAD work and your hand-rendering skills, so consider doing half your collections one way and half the other.

7. **Your résumé:** Many designers make the mistake of placing their résumés on the opening pages of their portfolios. If the recruiters have brought you in for an interview, though, then they've already seen your résumé. Maximize your portfolio's impact by using the first page for a really stunning image, and then include your contact information in an obvious (and attractive) place. Portfolio books often have a pouch in the front or the back—that's the right place for your résumé.

pinking: Cutting fabric with pinking shears (the ones with the zigzag blades), which prevents threads from unraveling.

8. **Fabric/color swatches:** Include samples of the fabrics and trims you would use in your garments. Cut and display them carefully. Either **pink** all your fabric swatches so that they're the same size and cut the trims to equal lengths or else create a readable collage with your swatches. Swatches can be glued directly onto the flats. (HINT: Use rubber cement).

9. **Croquis book (pronounced "croaky"):** *Croquis* means "quick sketch." Interviewers love croquis books because they show the breadth of your experience across different categories and different styles. Croquis books are full of ideas that go beyond your senior project (which will likely make up the bulk of your portfolio). Recruiters like to see how many ideas you have, and they like to see how your ideas change from beginning sketches to final presentation. Every designer goes through an evolutionary process, and a croquis book allows recruiters to peek inside your head to see yours. Some students use their croquis books as a combination of sketchbook, diary, memento book, and address book.

10. **Leave-behind:** Especially at job fairs, internship fairs, or other large recruiting events, you may want to leave more than your résumé. A leave-behind is an illustration or mini-book that will remind the reviewer/recruiter who you are after you've left. It's not absolutely necessary, but it can be a smart addition.

What to ditch

To keep your portfolio as professional as possible, leave out the following:

- Really bad or amateur photos of your garments. It's much better to just show great illustrations and flats.

- Fine artwork, personal work like nude drawings, or any student work that's not directly related to fashion.

- Unwieldy fabrics and sample garments that could come spilling out of the portfolio when opened.

- Graded work (unless you can erase the grade beyond any trace).

Avoiding Some Typical Portfolio Mistakes

- **Choose either vertical or horizontal layouts.** You want the reviewer's attention to stay focused on your work, so don't make them constantly flip your portfolio back and forth. And remember, although we read from left to right we tend to focus on the right-hand page more readily. If you've got a maximum of 10 illustrations or designs in your portfolio, display them prominently on the right-hand side only.

- **Use computer-generated lettering.** Unless you're a graphic designer and have studied type development, or spent some time doing serious street art or graffiti, hand lettering almost always looks amateurish.

- **Remember that neatness counts.** Take out any illustrations that have obvious eraser marks. Remember that grades—even if they're A's—mark your drawings as student work. Wite-Out and correction tape are great for correcting originals before copying, but they shouldn't be evident in your portfolio. And always make sure that Fluffy's cat hair has been completely brushed off your black portfolio case before you put it in your bag.

- **Edit carefully.** Don't include things that don't reflect your best work, and absolutely do not make excuses for your work during an interview. Never point to a piece during your interview and say, "Yeah, well, that was this senior project we had to do on swimwear and the teacher wasn't very good and I didn't really get direction so that's why the last two designs didn't really come out right . . . " If you don't like something in your portfolio, you have only two choices: Fix it to your satisfaction or take it out.

- **Tailor your portfolio.** Reviewers look for designers who share the company's sensibility and know their customers, so make sure your designs resemble the employer's aesthetic and target market. If you're interested in several different companies, buy a portfolio with removable pages and swap in different groups based on the company in question. If applying for a job at Ralph Lauren Purple Label, your work should reflect the luxurious and tailored look of the brand. Don't walk into that interview and show the Ralph Lauren recruiter a portfolio of hip-hop gear. In addition to considering the brand's look and price point, think about the fabrics and colors they currently use and adjust your designs accordingly.

- **Coordinate, coordinate, coordinate.** Make sure that all the work inside your portfolio is harmonious. Your work should look like the product of a single designer and the collections should relate to one another. If you've got a portfolio that looks like it was designed by the schizophrenic love child of Vivienne Westwood and Tommy Hilfiger, rethink your illustrations.

66 Make sure that your résumé relates to the aesthetic of your work. Don't present a portfolio filled with collections of dark, gothic pieces using rough, shredded fabric and then enclose a résumé with a cute little yellow bird motif. You don't want the employer wondering if the résumé and portfolio came from two different people. You're branding yourself with everything you show, and it should all work together to make a consistent statement that reflects your style."

—**Junko Carter,** Career Counselor
Parsons

4

BECOMING AN EXPERT

Now that you've written a killer résumé and figured out what area of fashion you want to work in, you need to do your research. Learn everything you can about the industry. The more informed you are, the better the candidate you'll become. Read, surf the web, build your professional network, and check into furthering your education. Here are some tips on how to fill your brain (and résumé!) with useful information.

READ, READ, READ

Even if you live in a fashion backwater, your local bookstore or library will have plenty of resources to help you in your career search.

Trade Magazines

You are what you read! In addition to keeping tabs on the major fashion magazines, such as *Vogue* and *Harper's Bazaar,* you should be reading industry publications that regularly post job opportunities. *Women's Wear Daily* and *California Apparel News* are the major industry bibles: Make them your new best friends.

- ***Women's Wear Daily,*** wwd.com
  A daily New York newspaper covering fashion business news in addition to regularly listing job opportunities. *WWD* now prints a weekly issue in Los Angeles, evidence of L.A.'s increasing importance in the apparel industry. Check out the wanted ads for New York design positions. *WWD* online is available through a subscription service.

- ***California Apparel News,*** apparelnews.net
  This is the chief resource for Los Angeles–based fashion industry wanted ads. The weekly Los Angeles trade publication covers the

business of the fashion industry. Its focus is on the West Coast, but more national stories and ads are showing up these days.

Recommended Books

Here's a choice sampling of current books about fashion history, design, merchandising, and clothing construction.

- ***20th Century Fashion,*** by Linda Watson, Firefly Books Ltd., 2004
  Published in association with *Vogue* magazine, this book by former *Vogue* writer Watson chronicles the designers, cultural influences, and technological advances in fashion through the twentieth century. Arranged both by decade and alphabetically by designer, this is a must-read for anyone interested in fashion history.

- ***Encyclopedia of Clothing and Fashion*** (three volumes), Valerie Steele, ed., Scribner Library of Daily Life, 2004
  A historian at the Fashion Institute of Technology in New York edited this major resource on fashion history (a whopping 1,453 pages!). The incredibly wide-ranging encyclopedia includes articles on various textiles, clothing styles, and construction techniques, as well as historical articles on famous designers and stylish fashion influencers. Many articles treat the cultural and social dimensions of fashion, and each entry includes a helpful bibliography. See if you can find this one in your library, since the entire set retails for over $400.

- ***Fashion: From Concept to Consumer,*** by Gini Stephens Frings, Prentice Hall, 2004
  This book describes the business side of the fashion industry in detail, with sections on color analysis, textile design and manufacturing, and garment distribution channels. Frings's book is often used as a textbook in college "Survey of the Fashion Industry" courses.

- ***The End of Fashion: How Marketing Changed the Clothing Business Forever,*** by Teri Agins, HarperCollins, 2000
  A writer from the *Wall Street Journal* looks at the business side of fashion design: manufacturing, retailing, and image making.

- ***Portfolio Presentation for Fashion Designers,*** by Linda Tain,
  Fairchild Publications, 2003
  This is a great guide for anyone considering a fashion design career. The
  author gives very detailed advice on how to assemble a great portfolio.

- ***Career Opportunities in the Fashion Industry,*** by Peter Vogt,
  Checkmark Books, 2002
  Vogt's book gives a broad overview of the many career paths in fashion
  and offers general salary ranges for entry-level to senior positions.

Logging On

In addition to regularly checking fashion magazine websites, be sure to
visit the following sites, which offer everything from job postings to in-
depth coverage of recent runway shows.

- **The Fashion Net,** fashion.net
  A cool site for viewing fashion shows and reading up on different
  labels. It also has a guide to the "green" fashion companies, which have
  environmentally friendly and socially responsible policies.

- ***Vogue,*** style.com
  The online home of *Vogue* magazine. This is a great place to check out the
  latest runway shows and to get industry buzz on the hottest designers.

- **The Style Council,** stylecouncil.com
  A site covering trend forecasting for men's, women's, and
  children's apparel.

- **The Young Menswear Association,** the-yma.com
  The website for a New York–based organization that awards
  scholarships and provides internship opportunities for students
  interested in menswear design. Schools participate by invitation.

- **Apparel Search,** apparelsearch.com
  Includes a free job board and a glossary of fashion and garment terms.

Check out the
fashion forums on
these sites:

thefashionspot.com

fashioncapital.co.uk

boards.core77.com

hintmag.com

fashion.meetup.com

Did we say *complete glossary*? The first six *R* entries in this vocab bonanza are *rabato*, *RFID*, *raglan*, *raincoat*, *rainwear*, and *rajah*.

NETWORK

People often find the idea of networking discouraging because they think they don't know anybody important or connected. Think of it this way: Your network includes the people you know personally—that's obvious. But it can easily extend to the people they know and the people *they* know. You'd be surprised who your friends, parents, and faculty members have in their Rolodexes.

What's the point of networking? To ask for a professional's advice on your job search and career path and to hear about their own experiences. Having a successful professional critique your résumé and give you advice on marketing yourself can be an invaluable opportunity in and of itself, but networking can also lead to you to other fashion contacts and eventually to real, solid job leads. Here are the basic ways to network.

- **Face-to-face:** Every day and anywhere you go, everyone you meet offers the opportunity to network. Whether you're in class talking to your fellow students or at an internship chatting with your supervisor, you're networking, whether you realize it or not. When you go to industry events, such as panel discussions and lectures, you're in the perfect place to network. Don't be shy about going up to the speakers afterward and chatting with them about what you enjoyed about their presentation and telling them a bit about yourself.

- **By phone:** Phoning is a great way to follow up with someone you've recently met or visited on the job. It can be daunting if you're calling a company that hasn't posted a job or where you have no connections. But it can be effective if someone has given you a contact name and number. Most people will respond positively if you say something like, "Hello, Ms. King. Tony Jones suggested I call you."

Professional recruiters know that 80 percent of jobs are found through networking.

- **In letters:** People get so much mail that this can be a tough sell. If you're going to try to get someone to open your letter, it's really wise to invest in great stationery and to be sure to start your letter by mentioning the name of someone who referred you.

- **By email:** Email is, of course, the most immediate way to network. Just keep in mind that professionals are inundated with emails, so keep your message short, sweet, and to the point. Think of your email as a cover letter, and keep it fairly formal in tone. Mention who referred you and exactly why you're writing in the first couple of sentences—don't take too long to get to the point, or your would-be contact's itchy trigger finger will be heading for the delete button. You can attach your résumé, but keep in mind that many people set their email to automatically delete messages with attachments from unknown senders. Set up your email program so that it sends you a confirmation when your message has been received; if it doesn't go through, try resending with your résumé pasted in plain text in the body of the message. Avoid using a funky, highly personal email address to send out anything job related. "Queendiva@hottmail.com" doesn't exactly scream "professional."

Informational Interviews

Informational interviews are conversations you have with professionals to learn about their expertise, seek career advice, and get more industry connections. The purpose of these conversations is to further extend your existing professional network and connect with more people who could offer you job leads. Often, even busy fashion professionals are willing to talk about what they do and how they got there. These conversations will often take place over the phone. If your networking works, and you get an informational interview, you should prepare for the conversation by doing the following.

- **Look at the company website.** Try to find a few things you could talk about that will show you have familiarity with the company. Find out about their hot new products. You want to come across as someone who's genuinely interested and excited about this person's work.

Everyone loves to be flattered if the flattery seems sincere—even the most successful people aren't immune.

- **Research the person you're interviewing with.** Using an Internet search engine, enter her name in quotation marks (this will help you get more targeted information). Go to the website of your favorite fashion trade publication and use their search engine to see if any articles have been written about your contact. Make some notes about your interviewer before you go into the meeting so that you can ask her informed questions about her career.

An informational interview is the opposite of a job interview in that you'll be responsible for directing the conversation. Don't show up and then just sit there, staring at your contact blankly. You can start with these safe-bet questions:

> » *How did you get your start in this industry?*
> » *What do you enjoy most about your job?*
> » *What do you see yourself doing in five or ten years?*
> » *What advice do you have for someone entering the fashion industry?*

Make sure you listen carefully to your interviewer's answers and be prepared to ask follow-up questions. You never know where a conversation might lead, so don't just stick to your list of prepared questions.

After the informational interview, rewrite your notes while the interview is still fresh in your mind—that means within 24 hours. This will help you gain the most from the experience. Write and send a thank-you note, as well.

66 Achievement doesn't happen in a vacuum. People that know this take the time to make industry connections early on, even before they know *what* they want to achieve. Start developing relationships now, before you actually need something. Because the fact of the matter is, people can smell desperation. They can see it in your face when you're just out to get something."

—**Angela E. Yeh,** President and Founder
Yeh IDeology, New York City–based design recruiting firm

Industry Events

Fact: You'll meet more fashion people at events such as conferences, seminars, lectures, and industry mixers than you will by sitting at home watching reruns. So get out of the house and watch your network grow!

GOING TO FASHION SHOWS

You may not be able to snag tickets to the next Michael Kors show right away. But if you want to attend a runway show and don't have an "in" with any designers, check out the fashion/style calendar in your local paper or regional magazine. There, you'll find information on **trunk shows** being held at high-end department stores and hotels, often for newer designers. Or, for a glimpse at the big-time fashion scene, check out Gen Art (genart.org), an organization that supports emerging designers and artists and holds massive shows throughout the year in New York, Los Angeles, Chicago, Miami, and San Francisco.

If you get a ticket to the show you'll be seated in rows alongside the runway, so talk to the people sitting next to you. Say hello, tell them your name, and pay them a compliment or ask them a question. If they say nothing, just smile and focus on the show. Hey—nothing good comes without a little elbow grease and embarrassment. But more than likely, they'll respond, and you'll have a brand-new contact. Who knows? Maybe she's an editor at your favorite fashion magazine, or maybe she's an up-and-coming designer who'd be willing to take you under her wing. She may very well be an accountant who won tickets from a radio station, but you'll never know unless you ask.

If you can't get into a fashion show through the front door, watch the trades and bulletin boards at fashion schools for volunteer opportunities. Being a **dresser** involves—you guessed it—dressing models. You'll follow the creative director's plan to make sure that the models are lined up in the right order and then stay on top of all the clothing changes. It's hard work, lots of fun, and it looks great on your résumé—plus it's great for meeting people.

66 As a dresser for Rodarte, I greeted audience members, dressed the models, and made sure the dresses were pressed and ready on the racks. It was a hectic, chaotic atmosphere, and the designers wanted everything to be immaculate. Crazy things can happen—like at one point, we ran out of shoes and had to give a model a huge pair that didn't fit. We had to put layers of Band-Aids on her ankles and about three inserts into the shoes to get them to stay on. After volunteering as a dresser, my résumé was really beefed up and I was able to get an internship in public relations at Michael Kors. I probably wouldn't have gotten that position otherwise."

—**Talya Shelley,** Design and Management Student
Parsons

COLLECTING BUSINESS CARDS

You should ask for business cards whenever you have the opportunity. Anytime you go to an industry event, lecture, or reception (and it should go without saying that you're attending every industry event, lecture, or reception you can worm your way into), you should be politely asking for business cards. When you get one, follow up with a letter or an email within a week of meeting. This note can be as simple as "Thanks for chatting. Nice to meet you." You can request a follow-up meeting for an informational interview if appropriate. Right after an event, gather up any business cards you've collected and write the date and event name on the back of each. Keep these business cards organized in a binder or put the information in an Excel spreadsheet that you keep updated.

FOLLOWING UP WITH CONTACTS (WITHOUT STALKING)

"Hi, Mrs. Smith. I sent you my résumé yesterday and I hope you got it. Would you call me and let me know?"—*Beep*—"Hi, Mrs. Smith. It's me again. I sent you my résumé two days ago and I wanted to talk to you about jobs there so call me."—*Beep*—"Hi, Mrs. Smith. It's me again . . ."

You'll be lucky if Mrs. Smith doesn't take out a restraining order against you—and you haven't even met her yet! Whether you're applying for a job or just contacting an industry pro for an informational interview, you have to be patient and polite. No one wants to help a pest.

- **Send a simple a thank-you note.** Send a polite note within one week of your meeting (preferably within two days). Mention anything specific you would like as a next step: an informational interview, a phone conversation, or a chance to further discuss something you talked about initially. Don't shoot for the moon— keep your requests reasonable.

- **Give them some space.** If you don't hear back after your initial thank-you note, you can follow up a few weeks later with an email or a phone call, but don't pressure them. You just want to keep the lines of communication open. They'll get back to you if and when they can.

- **Reconnect.** You can periodically reestablish contact by sending your contact a note, updating her on what you've been doing lately. Make sure to keep these updates relevant. Mrs. Smith at Bergdorf's doesn't want to hear about your new kitten, your new boyfriend, or your new tattoo. She will want to hear about your latest internship or your successful *Project Runway* application.

What's the number-one secret weapon in networking? Good karma. Always be kind to other people. Everyone from your employer's receptionist to your creepy fellow intern is part of your network. Treating others as you want to be treated is a smart investment in your future, not to mention a way to make you glow with all that goodwill-for-the-world business.

CONSIDER FURTHER EDUCATION

You're probably already groaning, "What, more school?!" But after going through the steps above, you may decide that you need more formal training before you're a truly competitive candidate. Further education can be a big commitment. The longer the program, the more time, energy, and money you'll have to spend. If you already have a bachelor's degree, you may want to consider whether an associate degree in fashion or a related field would help you make industry connections and gain some of the design or business skills you missed out on as an undergraduate.

When researching schools online, make sure your information comes from a truly independent source, and not one subsidized by the schools themselves.

Good Reasons to Go Back

- **You haven't completed a bachelor's degree.** Remember, most jobs in fashion will require a four-year college degree.

- **The degree you did receive was in physics.** If you've never taken any art or design classes, you may want to take a few now.

- **There are required job skills that you just don't have and that you can't learn on the job.** If you want to work in merchandising and you've never studied retail math, or if you want to be a designer and don't have any CAD skills, you should consider getting some training in these job specifications.

Good Reasons *Not* to Go Back

- **You haven't really committed yourself to working in the fashion industry.** Rather than jumping right back into school, try working in a retail environment, perhaps part-time. Find out if you like working with customers, dreaming up new clothing designs, or selling complete outfits with accessories.

- **You already hold a bachelor's degree in a related field, such as art history or marketing.** Consider applying for entry-level jobs or training programs aimed at applicants with your current skill set and education level before you commit to more student loans.

- **Your financial situation just can't support more school right now.** Even if you just know you have to take evening classes at a fashion school, the stress of juggling a job and school may overwhelm you if you're forced to make too many financial sacrifices. Build a financial budget, which includes a savings plan that will allow you to take classes further down the road.

A la carte option
Remember, it's not an all-or-nothing game. Lots of schools offer a range of stand-alone classes that don't require you to commit to a fulltime program.

Tuition Help

Going back to school can be particularly daunting if you're still paying off loans on another degree. Here are a few tips on funding further education.

- **Start with your public library.** Research scholarships and grants are offered by local businesses and larger corporations/philanthropists.

- **Call the schools you're applying to.** You'll be surprised at how many funding opportunities go untapped because nobody applies for them!

Financial aid officers should be willing to meet with you to discuss scholarship and grant opportunities, deadlines, and strategies.

- **Check into federal work-study opportunities and on-campus employment.** Sometimes, if you can find a full-time job at the school, your tuition fees will be waived and you can attend night school.

    The government also offers the following tuition resources:

    » Federal Pell Grant (limited to undergraduates)
    » Federal Perkins Loan
    » Federal Supplemental Educational Opportunity Grant (limited to undergraduates)
    » Stafford Loan
    » Subsidized FFEL or Direct Loan

    For details on qualifications and applications for these resources, go to the U.S. Department of Education's Federal Student Aid website at: studentaid.ed.gov/

What's in a name?

Diddy, JLo, Gwen Stefani, Jessica Simpson. First known for singing, acting, and living the celebrity high life, and now for their own fashion lines. Yes, the designs match their images. Yes, they undoubtedly have a lot to say in approving designs. But think for a moment about all the education required of a designer before you believe every name you read on a label. Diddy didn't just wake up one day and think, "I can produce a hit record. I bet you I can make a halter top." Celebrity "designers" usually have a whole team of professionals actually creating their lines—and you can bet that most of them have a degree in fashion design.

Evaluating Schools

Begin with the end in mind. Since this book is all about sparking your career, we're going to assume that your goal is landing a job. Figure out what skills or training employers require of new hires in your particular fashion field. Then you can evaluate potential schools against these criteria.

- **Class content:** They teach what you want to learn.

- **Faculty:** The faculty have experience in their field—maybe they only teach part-time and work mainly as designers, marketing executives, or PR gurus.

- **Degree:** The school offers the degree you need to get the job you want.

- **Job placement:** The alumni or career services office can give you a list of where their alumni work and in what positions. Don't just take a school's admissions department or website at its word when they say they have high placement rates. Google the school, do your own research online, and find out what's being said about the school in the media and by graduates. If you do talk with the job placement or career services office, ask what companies recruit at the school and what kinds of jobs grads end up with. Beware of schools that promise you the world. Some schools will boast that they place 90 percent of their grads, but often those students are placed in jobs that didn't require an education in the first place (e.g., retail sales jobs). Remember that if you want a design job, you need to make sure that graduates of the school actually get hired as designers.

- **Affordability:** The financial aid office provides assistance and can help you plan your debt load and payment schedule.

- **Flexibility:** If you must work during the days, the school offers night classes in the degree you want. Many four-year programs offer night classes, but some will require students to be full-time day students.

- **Internships:** The program supports for-credit internships at major companies or offers help in getting substantial summer jobs in the industry. The school is willing to provide you with a list of where interns have been placed in the past two years.

Designer yearbook

Even the best designers had to crack the books and suffer through finals in their day. Here's a list of some of today's top designers, along with their alma maters.

James Badgley, half of Badgley Mischka: Rice University

Manolo Blahnik: L'Ecole des Beaux-Arts and the Louvre Art School

Francisco Costa of Calvin Klein: Fashion Institute of Technology (FIT)

Tom Ford: Parsons (studied architecture)

Lazaro Hernandez and **Jack McCullough** of Proenza Schouler: Parsons

Marc Jacobs: Parsons

Donna Karan: Parsons

Michael Kors: FIT

Nanette Lepore: FIT

Stella McCartney: Central St. Martin's

Nicole Miller: Rhode Island School of Design

Rick Owens: Otis College of Art + Design

Zac Posen: Central St. Martin's; attended a summer high school program at Parsons

Narciso Rodriguez: Parsons

Cynthia Rowley: School of the Art Institute of Chicago

Anna Sui: Parsons

Rebecca Taylor: St. Catherine's College, Wellington, New Zealand

Vivienne Tam: Hong Kong Polytechnic Institute

5

INTERNING

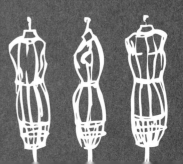

Getting an internship is THE most important thing you can do to make yourself marketable to potential employers. Recruiters often look at hundreds of applications as they search for entry-level candidates, most of which go straight into the circular filing cabinet (i.e., the trash can). A choice internship, prominently displayed at the top of your résumé, can earn you that all-important second look. Spending a summer or a semester working for free can give you valuable industry experience, not to mention being an excellent way to build your professional network.

DEFINE THE INTERNSHIP

What It Is

An internship is an opportunity for a student or recent graduate to assist and observe in a professional environment while learning how to apply his or her education to a real job. Internships usually require a minimum three-month commitment but can be arranged for as brief a period as a few weeks (say, assisting during a fashion show) or extended across several semesters. They're usually unpaid or offer a relatively low hourly wage or stipend. We know—it sucks. Get used to it. You know what also sucks? Making copies. Get used to that too. But immersing yourself in the professional environment gets you unmediated access to ideas, education, and networking opportunities, all of which will be invaluable when the time comes to take your career to the next level. Plus, if you're proactive about volunteering for any and all tasks, you'll get a reputation for being a flexible, willing individual—just the kind of person a company would want to hire for a fulltime position.

What It Isn't

An internship is not an opportunity for you to try your hand at designing a collection or running a department. It's also not a classroom, where you can expect constant feedback and attention, and it's *definitely* not a way to earn a lot of extra spending money. One of the most common complaints employers make about their interns is that they don't want to do basic jobs like book appointments, answer phones, and organize files. Remember, an internship is not all about you and your needs. It's a two-way street: Your employer gets help with their day-to-day operations while you get a chance to learn how the business works. Intellectual stimulation and creative satisfaction will probably not figure highly into your internship experience. But if you go into the job with realistic expectations and the right attitude, you'll reap major benefits.

Not quite ready for the big time?

It's the catch-22 of working in almost any competitive, creative field. You need experience to get a job—but you need a job to get experience! Don't throw in the towel just yet. Here are some relatively easy ways to jumpstart your career:

- Volunteer with the costume department of a local theater group. You'll probably start out mending busted seams between scene changes, but you might get a chance to sketch or help the design team.

- Work in a showroom, even for one afternoon a week. You'll meet buyers, learn about shipping orders, and build your customer service skills.

- Be a dresser at a fashion show. These Gal (and Guy) Friday jobs are easy to land and only last for a few weeks.

- Volunteer at your school fashion show, if they have one, or with a local charity fashion show.

INTERN IN DESIGN

If offered an internship in product development or production, take it. You'll learn about adjunct areas to design and expand your job prospects.

Interns in design rooms handle a wide variety of tasks. Some large companies, like Target, have highly structured intern programs that include weekly meetings, official mentors, and field trips. An internship at a smaller company might be less organized, but you'll probably be helping with everything from fittings to fashion shows. If you can get in touch with people who have interned at the company before, try to find out what their experiences were like. For now, the following are some common tasks for design interns.

Tasks and Responsibilities

- **Assembling mood boards:** Design teams put together mood boards to help illustrate and refine a season's design concepts. If the winter line is inspired by snow, you might go through magazines looking for pictures of snowshoes, snowmen, snowy owls, and igloos. You might collect paint chips in icy whites and frosty blues or get sent to find trim that resembles icicles or rabbit fur.

- **Tracking and recordkeeping:** Tracking involves following a garment through the production process. You'll be asked to keep records of all kinds—usually on the computer—and if you speak another language fluently you might be asked to correspond with vendors overseas.

- **Swatching:** Get out your pinking shears—swatching entails taking clean samples of fabric and trims and cataloging them for future use, along with their fabric content, washing instructions, and cost.

- **Sourcing:** Sourcing involves finding the best deals on materials such as textiles and trim. You may work with vendors over the phone or on the Internet or get sent out to patrol the city's wholesale shops.

- **Correcting colors:** When fabric comes back from the dye house, someone—often an intern with a demonstrated eye for color—has to use a specially lit box to check the fabric against the original color swatch. Even a white can sometimes be too blue!

- **Flat sketching:** Interns who have excellent drawing skills (and fluency in Photoshop and Illustrator) may create the illustrations that describe the basic shape of the garment.

- **Helping with fittings:** When samples come back from the sample makers (often overseas for big companies), the design team comes together for a fitting. The intern might hold the pins, tape measure, chalk, and notebook pad and pencils, handing them to the designer as needed.

- **Producing tech packs:** Factories need very, very specific instructions to properly produce a garment—particularly when the work is being done overseas. Interns may be asked to produce tech packs for the sample sewers.

- **Taking inventory:** Although computers track in-store sales, most companies manually inventory the merchandise or hand-count every item on the floor and in storerooms and warehouses. Brush off your abacus, because taking inventory is classic intern grunt work.

- **Designing graphics:** Students skilled at graphic design might be asked to create hang tags, labels, or imprints. If you intern for a company that does a lot of graphics on T-shirts, jackets, or hoodies, you might get to work on these designs.

- **Shopping:** Interns sometimes go shopping—or at least, they go to stores and take notes. You might get sent to check out a competitor's store, to see what's selling well. You might even get sent to stores that sell your company's clothes, to talk to customers.

66 Few places will trust you to take on important tasks right away. Take responsibility for your actions, be responsible, and show up on time. Be humble, be helpful, and always ask what else you can do to help instead of sitting around and waiting to be told what to do next. And remember: Don't make it personal. It's not all about you."

—**Aurélie Bonnefoy,** Intern
Carolina Herrera

INTERN IN PR

PR interns generally work the "front of the house." In other words, they're the ones stalking the lobby before an event, making sure everything and everyone is in its proper place. PR interns are people's people who enjoy talking up the show, looking after VIPs, and running across the street to get more water/exchange a pair of shoes/buy aspirin for an exhausted designer. Their motto is "Whatever it takes," and they say it with a smile.

New York Fashion Weeks take place twice a year—in February and September.

Fashion houses and public relations firms usually look for interns who have studied marketing or business. If you're interning in New York, you might start out assisting with runway shows during Fashion Week. PR firms host so many events during that period (including parties and press conferences) that they always need a lot of help. After you've worked on a couple of events, you could land a more extensive internship and assist with the below tasks.

66 My days as a PR intern mostly consisted of sending samples to magazine editors and celebrities. Not all that glamorous, but everyone has to pay their dues. It's like a rite of passage, and hard work does get rewarded. Grunt work is a part of any internship, but employers recognize those who are faithful with the small projects and don't complain. Once they see your commitment and diligence, your potential factor shoots way up."

—**Benjamin Setiawan,** former PR and Merchandising Intern
Michael Kors

Tasks and Responsibilities

- **Updating contact lists:** A well-stocked Rolodex is more valuable than gold. The more people you know, the wider the publicity you can scare up for an event or your client's new products. As an intern, it could be your job to update the database with current emails, addresses, and phone numbers.

- **Helping run tent events:** During market weeks, when new lines are debuted, designers hold receptions, parties, and, of course, the all-important runway shows. These events need name tags, sign-in sheets, extra chairs, double-stick tape, organizing of samples, coordination of models, and nerves of steel! Months before the event actually takes place, you'll be helping out with all the necessary preparations, such as writing press releases and organizing appearances for designers. If you can stay calm in the midst of chaos, you'll be adored.

- **Loaning samples to celebrities:** Fashion houses often lend celebrities garments in the hopes that they'll be worn to high-profile events, thereby garnering free publicity for the company as well as helping to cultivate a certain brand identity. As an intern, you could be asked to record and track products sent to and received from clients, as well as handle the actual delivery.

> **WARNING: Do not harass the famous people**
>
> If you're a PR intern, you can't get all goofy around celebrities. Don't ask for autographs, don't take pictures of them with your cell phone, and don't babble on about how sorry you felt for them during their highly publicized divorce. Only speak to them in your official capacity as an employee of the PR firm. If you truly admire their work, you can always offer a polite "I enjoyed your work in . . . " while showing them to their seat and leave it at that. Really. Leave it. The celeb—and your intern sponsor—will appreciate your discretion.

- **Handling press and advertising:** Interns are often charged with delivering samples to magazines, newspapers, and television tapings. If you're in Los Angeles or New York, you might also work at any number of small press events at your clients' flagship stores. You can expect to prepare lots of mailings (read: lick envelopes till your tongue bleeds), but you might also help write press releases, draft ad copy, plan contests and giveaways, and organize spokesmodel appearances and industry parties.

INTERN IN PRODUCTION

If you're thinking about interning in production, be strategic. Large companies and small ones offer the same kinds of pros and cons for production folks that they do for designers. The smaller the company, the wider the perspective you'll gain and the greater the likelihood that you'll get to do more than the standard-issue stapling and photocopying. At a large company, you'll see a smaller piece of the picture and you won't be able to take your responsibilities as far. However, these internships can be easier to land and, when you start looking for a full-time job, there's a greater chance that a larger company will have open positions.

Also consider what market category you eventually want to work in. Men's and women's fashions have very different production requirements, as do the various price tiers, and not all of your experience will transfer. So either start branding yourself early or, if you don't know yet what category interests you, try to complete a few different internships in various areas or look for a company that handles a variety of lines for different markets.

Tasks and Responsibilities

- **Basic clerical work:** Just like interns in every other area of the fashion industry, production interns handle a lot of general office duties. You'll send and receive packages, process invoices, and update Excel spreadsheets with the best of them. You might find yourself running around town delivering samples and picking up materials, or sitting in the office attaching piles of hangtags to garments.

- **Assisting at fittings:** An experienced or particularly trusted intern might help during fittings, when the design, merchandising, and production teams gather to review sample garments. You might be charged with taking notes or digital photos during these crucial meetings.

- **Gaining insight into the production process:** As an intern, no matter what your department, your most important task—besides being cheerfully available to your supervisors—is watching and learning what's going on around you. A good production person is an experienced production person, so absorb as much as you can while you're there. At this level, you won't be directly involved in any costing, negotiations, or traveling, but pay attention when your supervisor undertakes these crucial tasks and make sure to ask questions (when it's appropriate—not while she's actually on the phone with the factory in China).

LEARN ABOUT EXECUTIVE TRAINING PROGRAMS

Executive training programs are the ultimate fashion internship. These intensive, highly competitive programs (offered by fashion houses as well as department stores) prepare young professionals for jobs on the business side of the industry and provide invaluable experience for anyone looking to break into buying or merchandising. Trainees are usually recent college graduates who can devote a substantial amount of time to the job, since programs can last anywhere between three months to nearly a year. Another big plus? These programs are often fulltime, paid positions. Intensive training plus cash money equals a very good thing. You'll have the opportunity to continue your education while gaining hands-on professional experience, and you'll participate alongside a whole class of other young trainees, which means you'll have an instant network of professional peers (and moral supporters).

You can expect to face a slew of interviews and timed math tests if you apply, so get ready to really bring your game. As a reward for all your hard work and hurdle jumping, though, you get the satisfaction that comes with knowing you're being groomed for a full-time position upon completion of the program. The bad news is that these prized training programs aren't as common as they used to be, due in part to the mergers of many large department stores. But Federated, Bergdorf Goodman, Saks, Neiman Marcus, and Ralph Lauren are among the companies that continue to offer these excellent programs.

Areas of Training

Because of the comprehensive nature of most executive training programs, you can expect to have a much wider and deeper range of experiences than regular interns. You'll have your share of basic administrative tasks, but the emphasis will be on learning how the corporate world works. If you work for a fashion house, you'll learn all about your company's product, visiting warehouses and organizing vendor trunk shows and seminars. If that brand owns a store, you might spend time on the sales floor to learn about the principles of customer service. If you work for a department store, you might work on building strategic relationships with design houses or analyzing your store's sales in a particular area, such as leather goods.

As an executive trainee, you'll also learn about the following aspects of fashion business.

- **Trend forecasting and market analysis.** What's new? In the fashion world, that's not a pick-up line; that's the whole business of trend forecasting. Trend forecasters keep their eyes open for who's wearing their company's product and how those people are pairing it with other clothes. As a forecasting trainee, you might spend time on a college campus, at the mall, or snapping pictures at hot new nightlife spots. You'll also skim more magazines and websites than you could ever imagine, preparing to scoop the newest craze. Before you get over the top about this gig, you should know that it takes some numbers know-how to conduct market analysis. You'll have to study plenty of sales reports to see what's flying off the shelves and what's being nominated for "Dud Product of the Year."

- **Retail merchandising.** Products appear on department store shelves because a fashion company sales rep sold them to a buyer, who purchased them on behalf of the store. Retail trainees work with both buyers and retail merchandisers to decide how best to promote and sell the product. You'll discuss the key fashion themes for the season, the big product pushes, and strategies for displaying the product for maximum sell-through and customer impact. You'll strategize sales and promotions and you'll study the numbers. What's selling and what's not? Is a particular product languishing because of poor placement? If buyers are snapping up the new charcoal pencil skirt with the boucle jacket but never the sweater, you'll redesign the mannequins to reflect that.

- **Sales promotion.** It's the first rule of business: You have to get customers in the door before they can buy anything. Special sales, and the advertising that promotes those sales, encourages customers to come on down and scoop up the bargains. After the buyer has decided what he or she wants to promote in a direct-mail catalog (which will get sent to subscribers and frequent customers), the intern might be charged with sending samples to the advertising department, along with all relevant product info (retail price, sale price, colors). Sometimes retail interns will "shop" their own stores in another town to see what kind of customer service they receive and to make recommendations on how to improve it. These covert outings also give trainees the opportunity to witness real shoppers in their natural habitat.

- **Store operations.** Also referred to as "store management," this involves learning about . . . well . . . how stores operate. Trainees meet store managers and study the rules of customer service. They also learn about facility maintenance and the delivery, stocking, and displaying of merchandise. A trainee or intern might shadow a store manager for a day, following him around to see all the daily minutiae of his job. If you're studying to be a buyer, it's a good idea to learn about the flip side of the process and see what happens after you've selected the merchandise for your store. The more you know about customer demographics and buying habits, the better the choices you'll make when it comes time to restock the store. You might also accompany your supervisor to the warehouse or distribution center to learn how merchandise gets processed once the truck arrives.

66 As an intern at Bergdorf Goodman, I assisted the buyer in managing purchase orders and helped with magazine preparation. At a Chanel trunk show we did, I helped photograph models' looks, made the photos into boards, helped dress models, and organized clothing. Other projects I worked on included updating selling reports, preparing training materials for staff regarding new vendors and exciting products, and training new interns regarding the retail systems."

—**Farica Lam,** former European Couture Buying Intern
Bergdorf Goodman

GET AN INTERNSHIP

A great internship won't just fall into your lap: Landing an opportunity with a great company involves a lot of planning. You'll need a plan of action. Luckily, we just happen to have one here for you. You can thank us later.

Figuring Out Where You Want to Be

Your first internship is a great time to consider all kinds of options. It's probably just for a summer, so feel free to try out something new. Go ahead, apply to your dream company. At the same time, be open to applying for internships in lots of different settings, categories, and maybe even cities.

A small company will give you greater exposure to more aspects of the business and often comes with greater, more interesting responsibilities. However, the company may not have room to hire you once you graduate, and you might find that other employers don't always recognize the company name on your résumé. Bigger companies often offer perks such as housing, field trips, rotation between departments, and preferential interviewing for full-time positions down the line. Some people don't enjoy working in a corporate environment, though, where there can be hundreds of people in the building and as many as 10 on a design team.

Reality check: Working abroad

If your big dream is to work in Europe after graduation, consider the following issues before firing off an application:

- Does the company hire foreign interns? If so, does the company require you to file special paperwork?

- What kinds of government visas and work permits are required?

- Do you have the necessary language skills?

- Would the city be affordable? Are the exchange rates favorable for Americans? (Especially important when considering an unpaid internship.)

- Would the timing work out with your schedule? Much of France and Italy goes on vacation in August—plan accordingly!

- What are the employment rates like? When unemployment is high, opportunities for Americans drop.

Application Timeline

Calling up Donna Karan's human resources department on the first day of summer vacation isn't likely to land you an internship for the following Monday. If you know you want to intern somewhere, you need to start planning long in advance. Some of the most prized fashion internships are highly structured programs with strict application deadlines, often as early as February. Here's an ideal timeline for preparing applications. It's designed for college seniors, but it can easily be adapted for any job seeker. Just remember: It takes time to do it right.

FALL SEMESTER (SEPTEMBER–NOVEMBER)
- Develop your résumé.
- Talk to older students about their internship experiences.
- Begin researching companies where you might like to intern. Find out about their internship offerings and send away for materials.
- If you're in college, investigate for-credit internship options.

WINTER VACATION

- If you're a designer, work on your portfolio.
- "Shop" the pre- and post-holiday sales, looking out for the brands your target companies produce.
- Continue to research internships online.
- Make a list of the top 10 companies you'd like to intern with.
- If you can travel during the break, see if you can set up a face-to-face meeting with HR departments or internship coordinators at the companies you're particularly passionate about.
- Practice your interview skills (for tips, see Chapter 6).
- Develop a tracking sheet with opportunities, contact info, and deadlines (see the sample tracking sheet on the next page).

SPRING SEMESTER (FEBRUARY–MARCH)

- Finalize your résumé and print 20 copies on good quality paper.
- If you're a designer, finalize the sketches for your portfolio (see Chapter 3).
- Ask faculty members and former employers for letters of recommendation, if necessary.
- Meet with your career center advisors for access to job boards.
- Attend internship fairs hosted by your school or by outside companies.
- Check out online internship listings.
- Apply for internships, keeping your tracking sheet updated.
- Have a great interview (or two, or six . . .)
- Write thank-you notes.
- Get the internship!

Grownups can play too

Internships aren't just for college students. Consider getting one even if you've just graduated. You're probably thinking to yourself, "Wait a minute! I didn't suffer through four years of school just to do another unpaid internship!" But the truth is, it's a competitive job market out there, and sometimes it can take three months or more to find the right job. In the meantime—and especially if you're lacking in industry experience—a postgraduate internship is the perfect way to build and maintain your résumé while networking your way into a full-time job. Some internships, including most executive training programs, are only open to those with a college degree. Hugo Boss has a great internship (in Switzerland!) reserved for postgrads.

SAMPLE INTERNSHIP TRACKING SHEET

Date	Company	Contact Name	Contact Info	Activity	Next Step
2/28	School internship fair	Career Center	Shelly Rubin srubin@ school.edu	Portfolio reviews	Send thank yous
3/22	Fortune Cookie	Sarah Shin	(212) 555-8909 sshin@ fortunecookie.com	Emailed résumé	Call 3/30
3/22	Junior Heaven	Neecy Reid	(917) 555-8553neecy@ juniorheaven.com	Answered ad in WWD	Call 3/30
3/24	Junior Heaven	Neecy	See 3/22	She called!	Call 3/25
3/25	Junior Heaven	Neecy	See 3/22	Called	Send references
3/25	blu cru	Unkn	hr@blucru.com	Emailed letter	Email 4/5
3/25	wow@16	Karen G.	(212) 555-6666	Called	None—hung up!
3/30	Fortune Cookie	Sarah Shin	See 3/22	Called; no more interns needed	None

Finding and Applying for Internships

To find an internship you need to take full advantage of your personal and professional contacts. All that earlier stuff about networking? This is where it really comes into play. You never know when the guy sitting next to you in class will have a well-placed friend or relative. You'll also need to be a thorough and dogged researcher, using everything from Google to your career center to your favorite fashion magazines to dig up leads.

- **Network.** Tell your parents, faculty members, and the people you meet at fashion events that you're looking for an internship. Read all about networking in Chapters 4 and 6.

- **Use school resources.** College career centers have job boards, internship fairs, and internship notebooks, which are usually open to current students and alumni alike. They may also subscribe to Internet services. Employers sometimes contact academic departments directly for referrals, so make sure to let professors and career counselors know that you're available and looking for work. Find out if your school has an active alumni association or mentoring program that allows current students and recent grads to connect with alumni in their area of interest. Every alumni mixer is an opportunity to network, so come armed with business cards and your most charming, professional demeanor.

- **Subscribe to the trades.** *Women's Wear Daily* and *California Apparel News* often list summer internships. If you subscribe, you'll get the issue before it's available on the newsstand, which means you'll be able to beat the rest of the application crowd.

- **Get wired.** Fashion internships are all over the Internet. Individual companies often post opportunities on their websites, and you can find further job listings on Craigslist or Monster.com. In addition, there are subscription services you can use, which will send you targeted postings for a fee. Knowing how to do an advanced search can save you lots of time. Recommended websites include:

- » fashioninternships.net
- » fashioninterns.com
- » internshipprograms.com
- » jobsearchsite.com
- » google.com
- » newyork.craigslist.com and losangeles.craigslist.com

Coming up with too many hits? Try Boolean logic: Put quote marks around the search phrase and use the words *and, or,* and *not* between phrases.

- **Put yourself out there—a lot.** When beginning your internship search, apply for lots of positions. It's the only way to see how competitive a candidate you are. Don't wait to hear from one company before you apply to another, since it can often take a company over month to decide whether they even want to interview you.

- **Make sure you're eligible.** Be aware that many companies, especially large ones, require you to get school credit for an internship. If you aren't currently enrolled or your school doesn't have an internship class, you won't be eligible. Check out your credit options early to avoid a broken heart down the road.

- **Follow the three cardinal rules of job applications.** They're very simple, but you'd be surprised at how many people flub them:

  1. Make sure you meet the minimum qualifications.
  2. Follow the directions *exactly* as posted.
  3. Submit your application on time.

- **Don't be a pest.** If you really want an internship at Great Fashion Company X and they haven't contacted you since your interview, you can send an email a week later reiterating how much you enjoyed meeting them and explaining what you have to offer them as an intern. If you still don't hear from them, you can send another one the following week. If you still don't hear from them, stop! Either they aren't interested in you or they haven't gotten around to interviewing everyone yet. Maybe they're on deadline for delivery. Whatever their reason, three times is enough. Any more and you start to look desperate, and that isn't a good look for anyone.

66 I applied for an internship at Kenneth Cole and thought how lucky it was that I happened to own a couple Kenneth Cole shirts, all of them suitable for going to an interview. When I met the design director, he said, "Wait—is that us?" I proudly told him it was. Then he glanced at my belt and my shoes. He looked at me, unimpressed. "Those too?" I quickly learned that while all brands want to be aspirational, you shouldn't go into an interview wearing your appreciation on your sleeve, as it were."

—**Dan Strassburger,** Marketing Coordinator
Donna Karan

Interns are doing it for themselves

If you know you want to work for a specific company, run a full-bore campaign to get in there! Check their website weekly, order their annual report, shop at their stores every chance you get, pore over their ads, and Google them. If human resources is giving you the brush-off, do some research and find out the names of designers or other professionals on staff whom you'd like to work with and write them a letter directly. Write a brief but enthusiastic note about why you'd love to intern at the company and be sure to reference something specific about a recent product launch or campaign. Try getting a faculty member or career counselor to write you a letter of recommendation. For a design internship, make a mini-portfolio of sketches that look similar to the clothes they sell, and send these letters and this mini-portfolio along with your application. Remember, a company is more likely to hire full-time entry-level people out of their pool of interns, so if you want to work there full-time an internship can make all the difference.

Comparing Opportunities

If you're lucky—and good at what you do—you might have a few different options when the time comes to accept a position. Think about your long-term career goals when choosing your internship. If you yearn to design evening gowns for Oscar de la Renta, you'll be better off accepting an unpaid internship with a similar, high-end designer than taking a paid position with a mass-market brand or sportswear designer. If you find yourself in the enviable position of having to choose, consider the following factors.

- **The boss and the crew:** Hopefully, you got a good feeling about your potential supervisor during the interview. Otherwise, it could be a very, very long summer. In the best internships, someone is specifically assigned to serve as your mentor. They guide you through the procedures, are available to answer questions, and introduce you to the important people in other departments.

- **The clothes and the customer:** If you like the company's products, you're more likely to enjoy working there. Even if you're not interested in wearing them yourself, you should understand the taste and budget of the people who do wear them. Don't accept an internship with a children's-wear company if you absolutely detest the little buggers and the people who breed them.

- **Convenience and money:** Location is a huge a factor here. Are you going to have to spend a long time in the car, on a bus, or on a subway? If you have to move to another city to accept the position, will you be able to find a place to stay? (Most companies don't provide housing for their interns.) If the internship is unpaid, make sure you can afford to make little or no money for the summer. It's sad but true: Some people can, and some people can't. Talk it through with your family and consider your budget very carefully.

- **Your long-term goals:** Where you end up often depends on where you begin. If you intern with a hip-hop company you'll have an easier time selling yourself to an urban lifestyle company than to a women's bridge line. If you have a choice between interning at Phat Farm and working on the sales team at Ann Taylor, figure out which makes more sense for you in the long run. If you have a dream company in mind but can't land a position there, choose a company with a similar aesthetic so that you're more competitive the next time around.

- **The perks:** Sometimes the fringe benefits make all the difference, like a company cafeteria or paid parking. Maybe you've always wanted to live in New York City or you like the fact that the other employees look and dress a lot like you (or like the vision you have of yourself in 15 years). And though it seems shallow, you can't underestimate the cool factor. If it makes your heart flutter a bit to say you're interning at Calvin Klein, it might help ease the pain of an empty wallet.

SUCCEED AS AN INTERN (OR NOT)

Congratulations! You've landed your internship. Jump up and down, call your friends, buy a new outfit, and then make sure you *keep* that internship.

10 Ways to Impress Your Employer

Here are some rules for making the most of your time:

1. **Show up.** Be there on time, every day, ready to work, and well groomed.

2. **Be courteous.** That goes for receptionists and other interns, too.

3. **Listen and absorb.** There's a lot going on, so pay attention.

4. **Cheerfully accept all assignments.** That includes making coffee, running errands, or sorting three years of *Vogue* and *GQ* back issues.

5. **Dress the part.** Don't wait to be told that your outfit is inappropriate. Observe the way the regular staff dresses and adjust accordingly.

6. **Be proactive.** Ask how you can help out, and promptly tell your supervisor when you're finished with an assignment and ready to take on new tasks.

7. **Limit lunch to lunchtime.** And keep your personal business out of the workplace.

8. **Fulfill your commitment.** Don't leave two weeks early because you've got too much schoolwork or your family's going on vacation to Mexico.

9. **Ask for more information.** Get your boss talking about the design process, sales strategies, or whatever else you're working on.

10. **Find a mentor.** If the company does not assign you someone to work alongside, be interested in what others are doing, and your work relationships will grow.

10 Ways to Lose Your Internship (and Any Chance of Working for the Company in the Future!)

Sad but true: Talented people get good internships and then lose them. Some things you just can't do at work:

1. **Cry.** About anything.

2. **Arrive late.** Figure out the traffic patterns, the subway schedule, whatever you need in order to be early.

3. **Develop an attitude.** Your employer can tell when you're silently fuming, "I spent too much time at art school to be taking out trash."

4. **Call your employer an hour after you're supposed to be in to say you're sick.** Don't give her any opportunity to label you a flake.

5. **Call in sick more than once.** Unless you're violently contagious, that is. And even then, volunteer some extra hours once you're well again.

6. **Take home anything that belongs to the company.** Unless you have permission to do so, don't take anything out of the office that you didn't take in there with you.

7. **Take photos of the work you're doing without permission.** And don't even think about starting a "My First Internship" blog: People have been fired for less.

8. **Badmouth anyone in the company.** Or for that matter, anyone at a competing company. The golden rule? Don't badmouth anyone at all.

9. **Be embarrassed to ask for clarification.** Your boss would much rather explain something twice than have you screw up something once.

10. **Start an internship, then leave two weeks later because you've found a better one.** You can consider that bridge burned, so think carefully about whether you want to risk alienating a potential future employer (or colleague).

66 After you finish your internship, keep in touch throughout the year—months before graduating and going out on the job market—with recruiters and your supervisors from past internships, to stay on the forefront of their minds."

—**Ann McAtee,** Senior Executive Recruiter
Gap Inc.

EXPLORE ALTERNATIVES TO INTERNING

Sometimes, no matter how well you plan, you don't land the internship you want. Luckily for you, there are plenty of other good opportunities out there to learn about and observe the fashion industry.

- **Working fashion retail:** No matter what your area of interest, you should understand the retail side of the business. Working at a store will allow you to see how merchandise gets placed on the sales floor and how various factors affect real-life sales numbers. Perhaps most important, you'll get to interact with customers. If you take the time to listen to them you'll hear about what they love and what they hate. Maybe they love the new spring jacket, but the blue was too bright or they wanted inset sleeves instead of raglan. Maybe they wanted a matching vest, but it didn't exist. If you're a design student, you can try your hand at designing the missing pieces over your lunch break. You may never show your design to anyone, but you'll be training yourself to respond directly to customer feedback.

   If you're interested in working as a buyer someday, working retail at a store you love can be a smart strategy. Companies love to promote internally, because it means they're getting people who already understand the merchandise, the customer base, and the company philosophy. PR hopefuls can help stores plan and arrange contests, giveaways, and marketing pushes.

- **Working at a magazine:** PR wannabes can gain valuable experience working at a fashion magazine, even if it's not *Seventeen* or *Vogue*. If you can snag an internship in the editorial department, you'll start to learn what gets covered and why, which will come in handy when you're trying to get your own clients covered by the media. You might help with photo shoots, draft invitations to events sponsored by your magazine, or arrange reprint rights for photos. No matter what field you're headed toward, working at a magazine will help you learn how to talk intelligently about fashion. Be warned, though: Magazine internships are just as coveted—and difficult to snag—as a fashion internship. If you have a strong writing background and a strong fashion background, though, you could be a very competitive candidate.

- **Working in a fabric store/dye house/trim and bead store:** There are many smaller industries that support the design, merchandising, and PR sides of fashion. Working in any of them will give you a fuller, more nuanced understanding of the materials used to construct a garment. Learn your double-knit from your single-knit and your muslin from your linen from your lamé. Indulge your fashion OCD by cataloguing 30 different shades of blue denim dye. Surround yourself with ribbons, beads, and baubles and when the time comes to design your dream dress (or handbag, or shoes) you'll already be halfway toward getting all your material sourced.

- **Working at school:** Many universities and fashion schools offer summer courses for high school students. If you're still a college student and your school has one of these programs (and you'll be near campus for the summer), look into becoming a teacher's assistant, or TA. This is a particularly good option if you need to take summer classes, since tuition will often be deeply discounted for you, if not free.

International fashion escapades

If you want a job in fashion, you should take advantage of every opportunity to hone your skills. If you're planning on traveling somewhere over summer vacation or after graduation, make it a research trip. Take your camera, your sketchbook, and zippered plastic bag to collect small items like leaves and matchbooks. You might find inspiration for your next print from the pottery at Acoma, the flora of the Amazon, or the saffron robes of Tibetan monks. Maybe you'll discover a new love for 10-gallon hats and cowboy paraphernalia in Texas! Pay attention to foreign fashion magazines and advertisements and learn what sells both at home and abroad.

- **Administrative work:** If you can't land your dream internship, get your foot in the door by doing admin work at a fashion magazine, fashion house, or PR firm. You can start building internal contacts if you take a temp job or work as a receptionist or executive assistant. This may seem like a long, roundabout way to go but many bosses fall in love with great administrative assistants and are happy to serve as references for future jobs. Admin work is also a great opportunity to get a broad overview of the way a company works. Contact the HR department in fashion companies that you find appealing and see what's available.

- **Volunteering:** Who doesn't love free help? Try being a dresser for a fashion show, a volunteer in your local theater's costume department, or an assistant to the wardrobe coordinator on a film set. You might also try volunteering or working part-time in the costume design division of a major museum like the Met, or at a university like Kent State or FIT that houses major collections and ongoing exhibitions.

6

GETTING A JOB

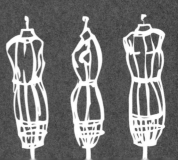

You're so ready. Classes—check. Ideal (but realistic) goal—check. Knock-'em-dead résumé—got it. *WWD* subscription, contact list, professional sounding message on your voice mail—check. Take a deep breath, because here it comes (drum roll, please): taking your first steps out into the big, bad world of job applications.

RESEARCH YOUR OPTIONS

Now that you've done your preliminary research and maybe have an internship (or two) under your belt, it's time to start applying for full-time jobs. When it comes to snagging that coveted entry-level spot on the fashion ladder, your research task is twofold. First, you have to keep your eyes open for job postings. Second, you have to do some in-depth research on the companies you're applying to—as well as the companies you *wish* you were applying to.

License to thrill

When a company hires another company to design and manufacture goods in their name, that's referred to as **licensing.** Warnaco Swimwear, for example, owns the license to manufacture swimwear for Speedo, Nautica, Anne Cole, OP, Catalina, Cole of California, and Michael Kors—although each of those companies has to approve Warnaco's designs before production. If you're applying for design jobs, figure out what other licenses the company owns. You could get hired by one company and end up designing for another, which could be a good way to diversify your design portfolio.

Finding Out Who's Hiring

Entry-level jobs in fashion open up all the time. Sometimes companies make it easy on you and post advertisements for those open positions. All you have to do is find them! Remember that a public posting will likely generate hundreds of applications, so make yourself stand out from the pack by immediately sending off an impeccably professional résumé (completely updated and tailored to the job in question, of course).

PUBLICATIONS

Check *Women's Wear Daily* as often as possible and, if you're interested in L.A.-based jobs, *California Apparel News*. You should also keep an eye on the Sunday edition of your local major newspaper, especially if you're on the business end of fashion.

Read the ads before you need a job. They show you what kinds of experience employers are looking for in their entry-level employees, which can help you fine-tune your résumé.

ONLINE JOB BOARDS

There are lots of websites with fashion industry job postings; these are some of the best.

- **Fashion Résumé,** fashionresume.com
  A résumé-matching service, which connects job candidates with potential employers. A résumé-review service is also available for a fee.

- **Infomat,** infomat.com
  A fashion industry information site and search engine. It features a career section where it lists its top 25 fashion job search websites, with detailed information and ratings on each.

- **Style Careers,** stylecareers.com
  A site that claims to be the largest fashion-only job posting site on the Internet. It has a searchable database of fashion industry employers, plus helpful résumé and interview tips.

If your school has an online job board or access to one, take advantage of it. Many companies list directly with schools, sometimes posting jobs that can't be found on their own websites.

WHAT WANTED ADS TELL YOU (AND WHAT THEY DON'T)

Want ads tell you the basic details of a job opening: its title, primary responsibilities, and requisite skills. They tell you how to apply, the location of the

SAMPLE WANTED AD

Luna
New York, NY
lunaapparel.com
United States

Assistant to Accessories Buyer

Luna, a Manhattan womenswear boutique, seeks an assistant accessories buyer to specialize in allocation, planning, and trend analysis. The ideal candidate will have a solid background in retail math, a positive attitude, excellent communication skills, and the ability to work in a high-pressure, fast-paced environment. Previous buying or trend forecasting experience a plus.

Responsibilities:

- Assist accessories buyer in all areas
- Keep records and enter data (knowledge of Excel required)
- Communicate with vendors on POs and receivers
- Work with buying team to ensure merchandise is allocated sufficiently
- Monitor store sales and make adjustments to distros as needed
- Communicate with marketing team on upcoming trends
- Help merchandise accessories in stores

To apply:
Send résumé and cover letter (with salary requirements) as Word attachments or PDFs to:

Lauren Sanchez
laurens@lunaapparel.com

NO PHONE CALLS, PLEASE.

position, and usually the name of the company. They may not tell you how much the job pays or what the hours are. And they don't say a thing about what kind of work environment you can expect. If only! Once you've seen an ad and think it's right for you, use your network to find someone who works there and ask for an introduction. Even if your contact works in production and you want to be an assistant buyer, they might know someone who can give you the inside scoop.

RECRUITERS

You might consider working with an executive search firm or recruiter to help locate job opportunities. You can tell if a recruiter is a good match for you if:

- The companies they represent are the companies you want to work for
- The ads on their website ask for experience you already have under "requirements"
- The recruiter responds quickly to your email or phone call

By all means, you should avoid recruiters who:

- Make you pay to use their services
- Make you sign an exclusive contract, barring you from working with any other service
- Promise that they'll get you work and then never return your calls

Recruiters have reputations too. Ask other people you know if they've ever worked with the recruiting company you're checking out, or pose the question on a fashion chat board. Try to get more than one opinion!

Although neither the authors nor the publishers of this book endorse any of these services, here are some of the biggest search firms in the fashion industry:

- **24/7 Inc.,** 24seveninc.com
  A bicoastal search agency specializing in placing fashion designers. There are both freelance and full-time job opportunities available, at entry and senior levels.

- **Solomon-Page Group LLC,** spgjobs.com

  A recruiting group that posts entry-level design jobs, primarily for mass market brands.

- **Project Solvers,** project-solvers.com

  A freelance and full-time placement service with a fashion resource section on their website.

Researching Specific Companies

Do your homework and find out as much as you can about the particular companies that spark your interest. Not only will it give you a better sense of whether you'd be a good fit there, it'll also prove invaluable if you're lucky enough to snag an interview down the line. If there's a company out there that you're really interested but that doesn't seem to be hiring right now, research it anyway. That way you'll be ready when there's an opening—and maybe you'll spot an opportunity that hasn't been advertised on the big job boards, giving you a big leg up on the competition.

- **Company websites:** Here you can expect to find an overview of the company's latest collections, their current aesthetic direction, and the breadth of their products. Look for features with the following titles.

  » **"Mission statement/Company philosophy":** Are they dedicated to diversity in hiring? Environmentally conscious production? Cutting-edge innovation? Think about what's important to you in an employer.

  » **"About Our Company":** You can learn all about a company's structure on its website, such as how many people it employs, what subsidiary companies it owns, and what larger holding corporation owns it. You can also find financial statements in this section (if not, look for sections with titles like "Investor Relations").

Under the umbrella
Look up some of the bigger holding companies like Limited Brands, Liz Claiborne, and Jones New York. We think you'll be surprised by some of the smaller labels they own.

» **"Employment/Human Resources":** Read up on the company's hiring practices. If you don't see a tab or button for job info, use the site's internal search feature to look for the term *employment*, or go to the site map and look for something along the lines of "Employment," "Jobs," or "Human Resources."

***

Surf warning: Don't believe everything you read!

No one's in charge of making sure online information is accurate, so you need to carefully evaluate what you read. Some websites have a clear point of view—often, because they're owned by a company trying to get you to buy their products. Be wary of any website that seems to be selling you something: Chances are, it is.

***

- **The company store (and the competition):** Take your show on the road and check out the company's merchandise in the real world. Let's say you want to work for Coach. Visit the Coach store, as well as department stores that sell Coach accessories. Walk around and take notes about the bags they're currently selling and the physical look of the store. Think about how you're treated as a customer. (Remember *Pretty Woman*?) You should also shop the competition in the same market segment: For Coach, shop Cole Haan and kate spade, which sell at the same price point.

- **Hoover's Online:** This subscription site has information on over 43,000 companies in 600 different industries. On hoovers.com, you can find all kinds of statistics about a company, including sales figures and the names of key executives. One of the most frequently asked questions in fashion industry interviews is, "Who do you think our competitors are?" Read up on Hoover's and you can rest easy that you'll know the answer.

- **Search engines:** If you type the name of a designer such as Zac Posen into Google's search box, you'll get more hits than you'll know what to do with. You can narrow your search by entering parts of your query in quotes, as in *"Zac Posen"* + *"design studio"* + *employment* and using linking

Let the Internet do the work for you. Sign up for RSS feeds from your favorite magazines or configure Google News to alert you whenever certain keywords pop up in the news.

words like *and*, *not*, and *or*. (Techies know this as a Boolean search.) You should also search for articles on any recent business developments in the company. If you want to impress a potential employer, show them that you're passionate about their product by being an informed consumer and job applicant. If you're applying for an assistant buyer position at Saks and the store just got a positive write-up in *WWD,* find a subtle way to mention it your cover letter and interview.

PUT YOUR NETWORK TO USE

While you're researching companies and tracking job postings, start by methodically reaching out to your network of friends, former work colleagues, and other professional contacts. This is why you built a network up in the first place, after all. Email every contact from every event you've ever attended. Start off with a simple, unobtrusive email: "Hello, I met you at the Trina Turk trunk show and you offered me your business card. I'm now looking for full-time work as a buyer. Could I send you my résumé?"

If you don't hear from someone, don't take it personally. People get busy, and many professionals aren't in the habit of opening unfamiliar email. Just send out more requests—eventually, someone will respond. If a query goes unanswered, you can send a follow-up email a week later. After two weeks, call the person with a friendly "hi" and ask if they received your email. Remember, though, that the golden rule of three still applies: If you contact someone three times and they don't respond, let it go.

Figure out an easy, standard way to track the responses you do get. (Lucky you! We've got one all ready for you. Check out the tracking sheets in the Career-Planning Workbook, page 271.) Use a spreadsheet so you can see at a glance who was interested, who wasn't, and who you still need to contact. If a potential employer responds with an email request for a résumé, send it right away with another short note. Don't go overboard with the gratitude, though: résumé, yes, flowers, no. Your note can include something along the lines of, "Please feel free to share this with others who might be hiring a PR intern." This is the secret to successful networking: not only getting in with the people you've met but reaching out to the other people they know, as well.

❝ ❞ Networking is essential for anyone in fashion. The best thing you can do to further your career while still in school is to build camaraderie with your fellow students. Help each other and stay in touch after graduation. The beauty of it is that the fashion world is very small and your fellow students often advance to positions where they are able to hire other people . . . like you!"

—**Tamara Albu,** Director of Fashion Studies Associate Degree Program
Parsons

Tales of the brave: Lazaro Hernandez

When Lazaro Hernandez of Proenza Schouler was still a design student, he saw legendary *Vogue* editor Anna Wintour on a plane and chatted her up. She went and got him an internship at Michael Kors and the rest, as they say, is fashion history. The lesson here is to let your enthusiasm shine and don't be afraid to take a few chances. Fortune favors the brave, so just let people know you love what you do and why.

Building Up Your Network

Keep expanding your contact list. Start making a conscious decision to seek out new people who might have job contacts.

- **Fellow interns:** Think beyond your supervisor. The other interns huddled around the copier with you could tip you off about that job opening at Polo. Introduce yourself and get their contact info.

- **On-campus recruiting:** If you're still in college, be sure to find out what companies are visiting campus in the spring. Even if they aren't fashion related, it's great networking experience. You never know how connected an HR person in business might be.

- **Career center staff:** Make an appointment with your university's career center. Show them your résumé and portfolio and seek their advice. Once in a while, the timing is perfectly karmic—you're there with a portfolio about leather design, and they just got a call from HR at Harley Davidson.

- **Alumni:** Your college probably has an online newsletter, a bulletin board, or maybe even an alumni mentor program. Contact the alumni office about how to hook up with other alumni in the fashion industry. Alumni office staffers usually know lots of people. And who knows: Maybe a fellow alum already works at your dream company. Alumni often have strong loyalties to their alma mater and, by extension, to you. Use them wisely.

- **Volunteer coordinators:** Sure, we've said it before. But it's worth repeating, since you're sure to meet more people who can get you a job by working backstage as a dresser than you will by hanging at the mall.

Tales of the brave: Heatherette

Heatherette is a hot young New York fashion label founded by partners Richie Rich, a former club kid and party promoter, and Traver Rains, a former horseback-riding instructor. Katy McColl interviewed them in her book, *Should I Do What I Love? (or Do What I Do—So I Can Do What I Love on the Side)*. Traver had studied economics in college but didn't feel Wall Street was a good fit. He met Richie during a riding lesson and the two hatched a plan to start their own clothing line. Neither had any designing training, but Richie had been making T-shirts that were "kind of derived from the Ice Capades, with sequins" and selling them at Patricia Field's boutique. Traver suggested they start a line together. They opened up a bunch of their favorite magazines and started calling editors asking them to show their clothes. It may have been naïve and awkward, but it worked—Richie happened to get hold of an editor at *ym* who loved their shirts. Richie asked to be put on the cover. Guess what? It worked. The next day, *NSYNC were wearing their T-shirts. Successful networking is equal parts chutzpah and making smart use of your existing connections. Richie told McColl, "My motto is, 'Don't ask, don't get.'"

If you want to start with baby steps, try just meeting one new person at every party or event you attend, and don't leave without getting a business card from your new acquaintance. Sometimes it helps to have a networking buddy who's a little more outgoing than you are, so they can give you a push when you're lingering mutely behind the potted ferns, clutching your complimentary crackers and cheese.

APPLY

Sad but true: Anna Sui won't be knocking on your door tomorrow. You can have the biggest network on the planet, but it won't do you a bit of good unless you send people information. Whether you're responding to an ad, going through an employment agency, or cranking out the cold calls, you have to put yourself out there, because that's where the jobs are.

Keep the following tips in mind while selling yourself to potential employers.

- **Follow the directions exactly.** Sometimes getting an interview depends on following simple, seemingly unimportant instructions. If the listing names a deadline, meet it. If they want four sketches, send four sketches (not 3 or 10). If they want the text of your résumé in the body of an email, don't get fancy and attach a PDF or even a Word document—your application will likely go straight into their desktop recycling bin. Many companies ask for résumés in this format to avoid the risk of a computer virus.

- **Unless requested otherwise, send a cover letter and résumé only.** Don't include a CD of your design work (they might rip it off) and don't send original sketches, because chances are you won't get them back. If the ad requests work samples, send read-only PDFs of your sketches: no finished work, no flats.

- **When sending out cold résumés, go ahead and send out a lot.** Send about 20 at a time. If you can't find 20 ads to respond to, send out the rest as cold calls. It can't hurt. After all, you're already not working there. If your résumé gets no response, don't be crushed. Just choose another 10 companies to target. If you're working through an agency, it will send out your résumé. Let the agency staff know you're interested in as many interviews as they can send you on before making your decision.

- **Follow your all leads, no matter how old.** If you found a promising ad while doing your preliminary research, send an email to see if the company has any new openings. As always, keep it short and sweet: "When I was researching jobs last May, I clipped your ad for a PR trainee. Now that I'm finishing school, I'd like to know if you're accepting résumés for any open positions."

Google unto others as you would have them Google unto you

You'll be Googling your interviewers; you should assume that they'll be Googling you, too. Do a search for your name on the Internet so you know what your interviewer will see. Analyze your profile on Facebook, MySpace, Friendster, and any other social networking sites you belong to. Are there any comments, interests, or photos that make you look, um, less than professional? Cleanse your online persona of anything that might turn off potential employers—at least for now. And probably for your first year on the job. And whenever you're looking for your second job . . .

Cover Letters

Lots of people cringe when it comes time to write a cover letter. But there's no need to sweat it; it's just a way to introduce your résumé and say a few well-considered things about why you'd be the perfect match for the position. It's not an autobiography, it's not a novel, and it doesn't have to be overly clever. Just follow this simple formula and you'll have a pain-free, professional cover letter ready to go.

1. **A greeting:** Always address your letter to a specific person, rather than just "Dear HR." Use formal business letter format. If you're

addressing your cover letter to Ed Brantley, use "Dear Mr. Brantley." "Dear Ed" only works if you know him well enough to have been to his house, and "Dear Ed Brantley" is just poor English. The only exception to this last rule is if the contact person's gender seems unclear. Rather than risk offending Ms. Terry Washington by calling her "Mr. Terry Washington," opt for the clunky but innocuous "Dear Terry Washington." Or better yet, call the company headquarters and ask the receptionist how you should address your letter.

2. **Why you're writing:** You're responding to an ad (From where? From when? For what?), or Katie Enders recommended that you get in touch, or you're following up on your conversation at the *Seventeen* event.

3. **Your current status:** You're just finishing school/moving to Dubuque/looking for a summer job. You're available immediately/after you graduate/next fall (for an internship).

4. **Your assets:** Tell them what sets you apart. (In other words, give them a sense of why they should hire you.) Offer a recap of your major accomplishments/awards/studies. Demonstrate your knowledge of the product, from retail experience, studying under a mentor, being a solid customer, or from your own research.

5. **Their attraction:** Explain what is it about the company or their products that makes you want to work there.

6. **The "fit":** Make the case for why they should hire you. Tie in your assets and your attraction to the company. This is your sales pitch!

7. **Contact info:** Let them know the best way to reach you. Provide your landline and cell phone numbers, as well as the email address you're using for your job search.

Easy, right? Turn the page to see how it all comes together.

SAMPLE COVER LETTER

Deborah Hong
47 Red Rock Avenue
San Jose, CA 95129

February 25, 2007

Ms. Grace Park
Intern Coordinator, DuPont Pontchartrain
560 Highway 44
La Place, LA 70068-6912

(1) Dear Ms. Park,

(2) I was pleased to see your ad posted yesterday on the Kansas City Art Institute job board for a textile design intern. As a junior in the textiles department, I am **(3)** looking for a summer internship, and this position seems most interesting. My résumé is attached.

(4) As a student, I have taken classes in color theory, surface design (including repeats), PhotoShop, and Illustrator. I have a passion for material and have worked during winter breaks at a fabric store near my home. I have spent the past four summers as a lifeguard, which has built my observational and communication skills. I am now ready to get a job within the fashion industry, preferably within textiles.

(5) DuPont has always been part of my life—as an avid swimmer, I spend the summers in suits made with your fabrics. The challenge of creating prints for stretch knits and neoprene is certainly interesting, and something I would **(6)** definitely enjoy. I am confident that my technical skills and my knowledge as a consumer would benefit your company.

(7) I can be reached by email at DHong@cox.net or by cell phone at (818) 555-1220.

Sincerely,

Deborah Hong

Deborah Hong

66 Don't send generic cover letters. The few I will never forget were so heartfelt—not sappy, but really thoughtful—not too long, and made me feel that this is the experience they really want at this time in their career. And there's always a way to find out a name to address the letter to. 'Dear HR,' 'Dear Recruiter,' or 'To whom it may concern,' has never impressed me."

—**Betsy Parker,** Senior Apparel Design/Recruiter
Nike, Inc.

INTERVIEW

If you've made it all the way to the interview stage, congratulations. This is the point that makes or breaks many applicants, but don't freak out just yet. You can easily ace an interview if you learn how to use it to your advantage. This doesn't mean being overly assertive or trying to control the whole conversation. You just have to be ready, behave professionally, and make a fabulous impression. Of course you'll be a little (or a lot) nervous. That's only natural. You can ease your anxiety, however, with a little thoughtful preparation.

Interview readiness = basic common sense + courtesy + composure. Sure it sounds easy, but it's amazing how many people fail to understand the importance of these simple points.

- **Research the company beforehand.** Be ready to talk about the product with knowledge and passion. Shop the stores and peruse recent catalogs so you can mention specific things you like about the current line.

- **Dress up a little rather than down a little.** For extra credit, try matching the company's aesthetic to demonstrate how well you'd fit in there. Just don't go all *Single White Female* and dress head-to-toe in the product. There *is* such a thing as trying too hard.

- **Show up 10 minutes early.** That way, if you're nervous, you can get a drink of water, fix your hair, or practice deep breathing in your car before you head inside. Make sure you turn off your cell phone before you go in.

- **Start strong.** When introduced to your interviewer, make eye contact and extend your hand for a solid handshake. Don't forget to wipe your palms first, and remember to smile.

- **Say "yes" to water.** If you're offered a beverage, don't get all fancy: Stick to the old standby. Water won't be too hot, and it won't make you jittery. Plus you'll have some on hand in case you suddenly get a dry mouth or cough. And if you spill it on yourself because your hands are shaking, you won't have to deal with the indignity of going through an interview with a brown, sticky blotch on your good suit.

- **Be short and sweet.** Limit each of your answers to less than two minutes.

- **Watch your mouth.** Sure, fashion is a cool, trendy profession. That doesn't mean that you can speak to interviewers the same way you talk to your friends. Avoid slang or language that's too casual, and don't say "um" or "like" when answering questions. (This might take some practice beforehand—it can be a harder habit to shake than you think.)

" I can't tell you how many times I've interviewed students for internships or entry-level positions who were discounted because of their use of casual words like 'stuff.' It's a poor reflection on candidates when they use vocabulary like that in a business setting. Also, make sure you use the appropriate industry terminology. It would be considered offensive if, for example, someone interviewed at an accessory company and used the word *purse* rather than *handbag*. It would seem like the candidate wasn't knowledgeable or up-to-date."

—**Kathy Schreiner,** Vice President of Human Resources
kate spade

Acing Your Answers

At a first interview, you won't suddenly be asked to choreograph an interpretive dance or calculate the circumference of the moon. First interviews are pretty standard, which means there's no reason you can't be ultra-prepared. Have smart, succinct answers ready for the following questions. Practice your responses in advance, so you don't fumble, blank out, or run out of the room in tears.

- ***Tell me about yourself.*** This is not a request for an oral autobiography, so don't start with where you were born. Start with what you like about the fashion industry and what you like about this particular company.

- ***Why do you want to go into the fashion industry?*** Aha! If you answered the first question as suggested, you won't get suckered by this one.

- ***Why do you want to work for us?*** You might like the company's product, or internship program, or the people who recommended you. Be ready to explain why you are enthusiastic about its product, style, or philosophy and what you can bring to the job.

- ***What inspires you?*** Hint: The answer's not "a paycheck." Tell the employer what genuinely makes you tick. What about its brand links to that passion? Be as specific as you can.

- ***Do you shop at our stores? What do you think needs improvement, or what do you think is currently working for us?*** Be honest but not *too* honest. Oh, and the answer to the first question should always be "yes." Make sure you've shopped the store (or the product assortment at another store) within the past week. Be ready to discuss the product and the shopping experience.

- ***Tell us about your design process.*** If you're a designer, an employer may ask you this as they're viewing your portfolio. Be ready with a thoughtful, precise answer. Being able to clearly articulate your aesthetic will set you apart from the pack, so practice answering this one beforehand. You don't want to freeze up on the spot and spout something dumb like, "Um, fashion?"

- **_Tell me about your internships._** This is when you can talk about how much you learned at that summer internship to show your prospective employer how willing you are to learn.

- **_Do you have any questions for me?_** Make sure you have something prepared for this inevitable doozy. Here are some good questions to get you started:

  » _What skills are most important to you in a new hire, and in this position specifically?_
  » _Is there a typical day here? Can you tell me what it would be like?_
  » _Who will I report to and what is the team structure like?_
  » _Can you tell me about upcoming projects I might be working on?_
  » _Does the company offer training for new employees?_
  » _What do you like best about working here?_
  » _How long have you been here, and what attracted you to the company in the first place?_
  » _You've probably hired for this job before; how have those hires been promoted?_
  » _What is the job culture and work environment like here?_

If you're interviewing with your potential boss, you might consider asking about her background and how she got started in the industry.

Don't

. . . Chew gum.
. . . Have a cigarette before the interview.
. . . Have a cigarette during the interview.
. . . Bring a portfolio so big that it knocks the interviewer's coffee over when you open it.
. . . Put down anyone (like a current supervisor or teacher) or any other company.
. . . Wear heavy perfume, makeup, or inappropriate clothing—no jeans and no exposed skin.

After the Interview

When you shake hands with your interviewer (after discreetly wiping your sweaty palms on your pants) and walk out that door, your interview is over—right? Wrong. Even after you leave the interview proper, you still have numerous opportunities to make a good impression on potential employers. Send a thank-you to the person who interviewed you. Some people like to send handwritten notes on nice stationery, but lots of busy professionals prefer to receive emails, which don't clutter up their desks. Whichever you go with, send your thank-you note right away (the same day of your interview, if possible).

SAMPLE THANK-YOU NOTE

Dear Ms. Regatta,

Thank you for taking the time to talk with me yesterday afternoon about interning at Nautica. I've always been inspired by the clothes, and now I'm inspired by the company and the people as well. I particularly enjoyed seeing the colorways for Fall '07 and the mock store. After our talk, I am even more excited about an opportunity to work with your merchandiser. I can be reached by phone or email. I look forward to exploring this opportunity further.

Sincerely,
Juanita Martinez

(646) 555-9056
JMartinez@geemail.com

Making a Decision

Wait until all offers come in before you decide which job you'd like to take. If you get offered a great job but have already accepted another, think carefully before you bail. It's a small world out there, and you can spoil your reputation if you handle the situation poorly. When weighing options, consider the following questions.

- **What will you be doing all day?** If the tasks themselves don't interest you, you'll need some other motivation for working there, whether it's the potential for advancement or the prestige of the company.

- **Who's on your team?** Your coworkers and your supervisor make a huge difference in your work world.

- **What do they make?** If you can't get excited about the company's products, it'll be much harder to get excited about designing, promoting, or selling them.

- **Where is it?** Location matters. If family needs you in Ohio, it could be hard to take a job in New York—or vice versa.

- **What next?** In a small company you might rise quickly to the top (while still doing all your own paperwork). In a large company there may be more opportunities for advancement, but it'll probably take you longer to reach your ideal position.

- **What comes with the deal?** Benefits, including health care, paid vacation, profit sharing, and employee discounts, often cost the company up to 30 percent of your salary.

- **Is the money comparable?** Notice that we list money last. We know it's important, but if the money is comparable, think carefully about the other parts of the offer. And if the money isn't comparable, you should still be thinking about the other parts of the job first. Life's too short to do something you're not excited about, with people you don't get along with, in a company whose products make you yawn uncontrollably.

If you do need to turn down a job, don't burn your bridges. Be polite and gracious and thank your contact for his or her time and attention. Remember, everyone you meet in the industry has the potential to be a future colleague (or boss).

7

NAVIGATING YOUR FIRST JOB

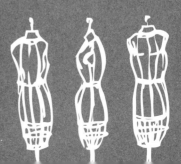

So you've landed your dream job (or the job that leads to your dream job). But don't think you can just rest easy now. Your first job sets you up for the next job and the job after that. The fashion industry may seem large, but since everyone moves in the same circles it can actually be very small in practice. People talk. At this stage, your attitude and reputation are just as important as your work ethic. Read on for tips on surviving—and thriving—in your first job.

BRUSH UP ON WORK BEHAVIOR 101

Common courtesy and common sense should be your constant guides, especially important when you begin your professional career. As you move up the professional ladder your reputation will precede you, so make sure it looks spotless.

66 Be eager and humble. Try to be a sponge and soak up as much as you can, even if it doesn't pertain to the department that you're working in. The faster you understand the big picture, the better off you'll be in the long term. Don't be afraid to speak up or have an opinion, and remember that no question is too small. The only stupid question is the one that doesn't get asked."

—**Andra Newman,** Director of Recruiting
J. Crew

The Basic Rules

Whether working in a design room, at a PR firm, or on the floor of a trade show, the basic rules of professional behavior apply.

- **Be there.** Being there means a whole lot of things. Be there every day. Be there on time. Be on task (i.e., don't daydream). Be fully present at meetings—and be there without your cell phone.

- **Be careful what you say (or type).** Mom was right: If you can't say something nice about someone, don't say anything at all. Here's a modern corollary to that rule: Never write anything in an email that you wouldn't mind seeing on the side of a bus. Email may seem like a casual way to communicate, but anything you write in an email can be shared with countless other people or forwarded without your knowledge to a boss or supervisor. Your email etiquette reflects on you as a potential employee, so keep it neat, professional, and to the point. Remember that many companies regularly monitor their employees' email and Internet activity, so refrain from cursing or gossiping on the company line.

- **Volunteer to help.** When it comes time to work an event, schlep a garment to the other side of town, or get a big order out to the stores, roll up your sleeves and pitch in. Ask first, though—there's nothing more annoying than unwelcome meddling. Make sure to clear it with your boss too, in case he or she needs you for something else more pressing.

- **Tidy up.** Leave your work area clean every day. Not only does it keep you organized, but it also shows that you have respect for your job, your workplace, and your coworkers. If others need to pick up where you left off, they can easily find the materials they need. Plus, you'll get a jump on the next day.

- **Keep your personal life personal.** Especially during the first couple of months, keep your personal life separate from your work life. Your coworkers don't need to know about your roommate's hygiene habits or the creepy blind date you ditched last week. When you start making friends, you can talk about your other interests—including fashion— over lunch or after work.

- **Be friendly.** A smile goes a long way. So do "hello," "please," and "thank you."

66 The fashion industry has a reputation for being catty. I'm not sure if it was because I was the new person or if it was just the learning curve, but for my first six months I felt like everyone was trying to catch me dropping the ball. So many conversations ended in, 'Well, I never said that,' or 'I never agreed to this. I learned to follow up phone conversations with email recaps, to require signatures on *all* projects, and to archive and cc my boss on any important emails. I know it sounds insanely cynical to need a paper trail, but forwarding a coworker's written consent quickly ends the 'he said, she said' game. And as an added bonus, it makes you look well organized."

—Anonymous

10 Ways to Make Your Boss Rue the Day He Hired You

1. **Don't dress the part.** If you work at kate spade, even as an intern, don't show up in torn jeans and neon Converse. Match the company's aesthetic as much as you can.

2. **Begrudge the drudge.** Turning up your nose at basic tasks like filing papers or labeling boxes is a surefire way to lose your boss's good favor.

3. **Gossip about anyone.** Especially your supervisor.

4. **Date anyone at the office.** Especially your supervisor.

5. **Goof off at work.** Spend your day hopping between Gmail, your BlackBerry, and your cell phone and you'll soon find yourself with a lot more time for personal interactions—because you won't have a job.

6. **Insist on leaving the office at 6 P.M. on the dot.** You should strike a healthy work/life balance, but if a fire needs to be put out you should be rolling up your sleeves rather than shoving your wristwatch in your boss's face.

7. **Go around your supervisor's or coworkers' backs on anything.**
Otherwise you can get a reputation for being disloyal, clueless, or
untrustworthy.

8. **Chat online about your workplace or upcoming product
launches.** Exercise caution and discretion and when in doubt, zip it.

9. **Take office property home without permission.** Don't be the fool
who sneaks the ultra-exclusive launch party guest list out of the office
and then leaves it on the bus.

10. **Cry.** This is not your classroom, not your home, and not your shrink's
couch. Wait till you get home.

MANAGE YOUR OFFICE RELATIONSHIPS

Office politics can often take up more time and energy than your work
assignments. Establish appropriate relationships early and you'll have a
much easier time avoiding any social quagmires.

You and Your Boss

Your relationship with your first boss can be one of the most important relationships of your life. Not only will you learn a lot, but he or she can also
prove an invaluable source of advice and support as you advance in your
career. At your first job, your primary responsibility will be helping your
boss meet his or her objectives. Whether that means delivering a sample
to a magazine, having the notes ready for a fitting, or keeping the client
database in order, your supervisor will count on you to help ensure that
things run smoothly. Proving your abilities as a competent assistant is the
first step toward acquiring responsibilities and authority of your own.

At first, you should plan on spending a lot of time observing your
boss's behavior. You'll learn how often she comes in early, works late,
eats at her desk, calls in sick, raises her voice, has team meetings, and

praises her employees. Once you've worked with the same supervisor for a few months you'll probably fall into a groove where you can anticipate what she wants and how she wants it. In the meantime, keep these tips in mind.

- **Get to know his or her communication style.** Every supervisor communicates with employees a little differently. Some like everything documented in emails or memos. Some feel ambushed when you pop into their office unannounced with an update. Some can look at a sketch and tell you in 30 seconds if it's right or wrong, while some will want to sit and talk out their ideas with you. Take mental notes about how your boss works and shift your communication style accordingly.

- **Double-check your work.** Carpenters have a saying: "Measure twice, cut once." In the fashion industry, that mantra means double-checking your math, your specs, and your spelling. Your boss isn't your teacher. He won't have the patience to review your work and give you endless feedback and opportunities for revision. When you submit a report or project, always edit your work carefully and check it for mistakes. And remember, presentation counts! Check that whatever materials you give your boss—market analyses, sales reports, color corrections, or press clippings—are neat and in order.

- **Help your boss look good whenever possible.** If your boss is on his way to a meeting and you know he should have the samples/specs/story/photographs, politely stop him before he walks into the conference room. Ask him if he has everything he needs. If he says yes, ask a more direct question, such as, "Do you have the binder with the sales reports?"

- **When you don't know something, admit it.** Usually a simple "I don't know" will do. Whenever you can, follow up that admission with a specific offer, such as "I can find out by this afternoon," or "I expect those numbers to be here by Thursday." If you have enough information to make an educated guess, do so, but if you don't have a clue, don't fake it. It'll only get you in trouble later.

- **Say "yes" whenever possible.** Deadlines are crucial in this industry and people get jammed up all the time. Your boss may get a request from another department asking for extra hands. If she asks you to pitch in, do it, but be clear about your other responsibilities. Say something like, "I'd be happy to help them with their sales report, but that does mean I'll have to push off my August numbers for now." Ask her what her priority is at the moment, and how you should prioritize your work accordingly.

Finally, try to remember that bosses are people too. They make mistakes, lose their tempers, and get overworked and overwhelmed. When you think your boss is acting unfairly toward you, stop and think. What could be motivating her behavior? Have I seen her act like this before? If so, when? No need to hang up your shrink shingle here, just develop a little empathy. When things go wrong and the boss gets upset, think about her goals, motivation, and risk in the current situation and you'll have walked a mile in her Jimmy Choos.

" I once had a boss who was just like Miranda in *The Devil Wears Prada*. Everyone feared her, and she loved it. She would say things really fast and not let you answer her and then expect you to know exactly what she wanted, which was often a personal errand: "See this hairclip I'm wearing? No, don't stare at it! Just go to Bergdorf and get me one just like it!" And she demanded at least 10 decaf iced coffees daily, so it wasn't unusual to see two interns standing in her office, each balancing a tray of coffee. An intern got fired once just because she brought her a caffeinated coffee."

—Anonymous

CROSSING THE GENERATION GAP

The current generation of entry-level job seekers (often referred to as "the millennials") shares some distinctive expectations when it comes to the workplace and their careers. Millennials assume the inalienable right to speak their minds freely, and they anticipate that their opinions will be heard and valued. They expect immediate gratification and a fast career progression, and they usually believe a college education to be a guarantee of job placement.

We get it. You want to have your voice heard and you want your opinions to be respected. But the older generation—the Gen X-ers and baby boomers who are likely your bosses and coworkers—may view younger workers as impatient and entitled. Don't give them an opportunity to write you off because of surly behavior.

If you feel like your boss is out of touch, join the club. Groaning about the historical relic who supervises you is practically a requirement of being a young employee. But when working with older colleagues, consider how much they know. They probably feel like they've paid some serious dues, since many of them will have spent years getting to their current positions. They want to feel respected by new hires, so make a point of asking their opinions. Even if you're truly exceptional (and of course, you are, aren't you?) there are still structures in place regarding promotions and project assignments. Respect that process. Be patient, polite, and humble in the way you express yourself.

WHEN YOUR BOSS IS OLD ENOUGH TO BE YOUR . . . SISTER?

On the other hand, you might end up with a boss who's very close to you in age. Maybe she graduated from your alma mater, just a few years ahead of you. (This is especially likely if you went to a design school, since there are fewer of them and their alumni are highly concentrated in the industry.) The good news: You may find it easier to communicate with a younger boss, and you'll probably have more in common with her than you would with someone significantly older. The challenge: It's easy to see your boss as a peer and forget to treat her like a supervisor. You may love the idea of working with a cool boss you could kick back a few with after work. But all friendships can go sour, and the last thing you want is a boss who's miffed that you didn't show up last weekend to help her move into her new apartment.

No matter how old your boss is, he's in charge and should be treated as such, particularly since he has so much influence over your work environment. Don't spend too much time chatting about your personal life. The weird blind date you had last week, the roommate who keeps you up all night with his blaring trance music, your parents' divorce—save those for happy hour with your friends and keep some personal distance at the office. Ditto with more serious topics like mental health or substance abuse.

Don't assume that private confessions will stay private until you have a longstanding relationship with your supervisor.

Even if your boss is old enough to be your parent, she may still be a chatterbox who wants to share details of her life with you every morning over coffee. This is tricky. You don't want to give the impression of being uninterested in her life, but you also need to establish an appropriately professional relationship with her. Don't get drawn into gossip or try to give her advice on her personal life. If she's going on and on about, say, her sex life, just smile or nod politely and chuckle when prompted. Don't by any means try to top her with something like, "If you think *that's* bad, let me tell you about this one summer . . . "

Staff Hierarchies and Office Politics

Keep your nose clean, kid. Business means business politics, whether you're at a small, family-owned boutique or a billion-dollar retailer. When you arrive at a new company, keep in mind that there's probably a complex system of group dynamics already in place. Tread lightly at first. Your discretion and caution in the early months will pay off in spades later.

- **Stay away from drama.** People complain about their coworkers—it's a fact of life. Do your best to stay neutral. It's okay to say, "Maybe I'm not the best person to hear this," or "I'm sure you're in a difficult situation" to evade a potentially uncomfortable (and unwise) discussion. Don't repeat negative comments. This may seem difficult when things are going badly, but keep in mind that gossip spreads quickly. If you get the reputation for being indiscreet, it can affect your chances for promotion down the road.

- **Listen and learn—from everyone.** You'll quickly figure out who has formal power (the people who run the company) and who has informal power (the people who carry a lot of influence). Respect both. If an assistant designer who's been there a year longer than you suggests you do something a certain way, be respectful of her seniority. Listen to her opinions and understand that you can learn from everyone at the company, not just your boss.

- **Follow procedures.** Especially when it comes to reports, complete projects correctly and on time and you'll stay on everyone's good side. Get a planner or calendar and clearly mark all your important due dates in it. There's nothing worse than missing a deadline with a new boss. If you need help with a report, see if a colleague will give you some quick feedback or ask your boss to review an early draft or outline.

- **Don't expect everything to be fair.** It might seem to you that some people get more opportunities and recognition than others. Don't focus on them: Focus on doing a great job and being a good team member. If you don't think your work is being properly acknowledged, find an acceptable (but non-obnoxious) way to keep your supervisor updated on your current projects and accomplishments. For example, you could prepare a personal status report and share it with your boss in a weekly email or at regularly scheduled staff meetings.

- **Get a rep for being a team player.** No sports equipment necessary—this is about attitude. When you finish your work tell your boss that you're ready for more. He'll give you another assignment, which may involve anything from helping the sales department crunch numbers for a big report, to taking a package of sample embroidery to the post office for the design team, to photocopying documents for a marketing meeting. This all helps you, because when it comes time for a promotion, people all over the company—not just the ones in your department—will know you as a hard worker and an enthusiastic team player.

- **Check your ego at the door.** You may have graduated cum laude from a prestigious college or spent a summer in Paris working for Chanel. But now that you're a full-fledged member of the work force, guess what? No one cares what you did before you joined the company. The only things people want to know now are: Did you do your job? Did you make your numbers? Did the boss get what she needed from you for the next meeting? In other words, don't decorate your workspace with your awards . . . until you start winning them from your company.

> **To blog or not to blog?**
>
> These days, it seems like everyone and his mother has a blog. But unless your ultimate goal is to land a book deal for your spicy tales of behind-the-scenes fashion drama, don't even think about applying for that Blogger.com account. It's way too hard to keep a diary (which is essentially what a blog is) without spilling some secrets. If you mention something sensitive—such as your boss's wicked diva behavior or Justin Timberlake's RSVP to your spring runway show—you could get in deep trouble. Likewise, it might be really tempting to share the cute concept you're working on for the new knitwear line, but if it's company work then it's company property, and your employers don't want you scooping them. Everyone has a horror story about someone indiscriminately blogging something that came back to bite them in the backside. Want a long career in fashion? Spill your guts in an old-fashioned diary and hide the key.

Mixing Business with Pleasure

Scary but true: As a full-time employee, you'll spend most of your waking hours at work. Naturally you're going to want to form friendships with the people slaving away beside you. Work friends can be wonderful sources of support and encouragement, and when you have one of those frustrating days that makes you want to stab your own eyes out with a pair of pinking shears they'll be there to talk you down off the ledge. Work relationships, though, are a special breed of friendship and should be treated accordingly. When you're all on the same payroll—and potentially jockeying for the same promotions—things can get sticky if you're not careful about separating your work life from your personal life.

> 66 When I'm working long hours and losing steam, staring at specs that need to get out to the factory and a looming early-morning conference call with overseas vendors, reaching out to my other friends in the fashion industry gives me perspective. It makes you feel better to know that you're not the only one still at work at 10 P.M., paying your dues. "
>
> **—Jenny Fong,** Womenswear Designer
> Akademiks

10 Things to Avoid at the Company Holiday Party

1. Sitting in the corner with your small team and ignoring everyone else.

2. Hanging on your date like cling wrap.

3. Forgetting to introduce your date to your boss.

4. Having that date be someone from the office.

5. Gossiping about people's clothes or dates.

6. Drinking so heavily that you end the night slumped on the bathroom floor.

7. Wearing something too small, too tight, too short, or too see through.

8. Dancing like a crazy person.

9. Slipping outside for a little "extra party fun" in the form of recreational drugs.

10. Bringing work for your boss to look at.

SOCIALIZING WITH COWORKERS

Whether you were a Mean Girl in high school or a chess club devotee, you probably remember how cliques work. Guess what? They're not just for kids. Large groups always manage to separate into little tribes, so don't feel nervous about striking up close friendships with a few like-minded colleagues. Just be careful: Cliques lead to a feeling of intimacy, which lead to indiscreet gossip sessions, which lead to all kinds of nasty consequences. Your office buddy's loose lips could not only get you in trouble—intentionally or otherwise—but you don't want to get a reputation around the office for being cliquey or snobbish. Your fashions should be exclusive and off-limits, but not your personality. So don't make the break room your little clubhouse. Take down the "Designers Only: All Else Keep Out!!" sign and make an effort to get to know the folks in other departments. Start by chatting up someone whose personal style you admire or whom you keep bumping into on the early-morning elevator ride. And remember: If you make friends with people in other departments, it can really help to grease the wheels in professional situations. If you goof before a meeting and suddenly find yourself with the wrong set of sales forecasting statistics, you can run over to merchandising and ask them to run you some figures right away—which they're far more likely to do if they like you in the first place.

When you make all these wonderful new work friends, chances are you'll spend some time with them outside the workplace. Just remember that you can't let your hair down with your coworkers the same way that you can with your old college roommates. When sharing cocktails, spare them the intimate details of your sex life and sordid pre-fashion past. Also, try to keep things mum when you get back to the office. Don't go on and on about the hilarious happy hour you hit with your pals from PR, because someone's bound to feel slighted for being left out of the fun. And as funny as it was to watch Lauren from the women's tops department try to hit on that bouncer last Saturday night, Lauren might not feel too kindly toward you for sharing that news during lunch hour.

The last minefield: the office party. Sure, your bosses want you to relax and enjoy yourself, and they want you to bond and befriend your coworkers. But any time you're at a company-sponsored event, remember that it's just that: company sponsored. Treat it as an extension of the regular business day that happens to come with finger foods and an open bar. Stay sober, smile at people, and whatever you do, don't tell Chad from wovens what you *really* think of his boss's new trophy wife.

DATING AT WORK

Love is in the air . . . but not in the office. If you just can't help yourself and you fall madly in love (or, let's face it, lust) with a coworker, take a moment to consider what you're getting into. Sure, it'd be nice to end a long night of drafting press releases with a little how-do-you-do in the supply closet. And if you somehow end up marrying this person, you will definitely have an excellent story for the wedding announcement pages. But how many twentysomethings do *you* know who can make consistently responsible choices when it comes to relationships? Office crushes can help make a slow Wednesday go a little faster, but struggle with your hormones and try to keep it from developing into a full-on fling, especially if you have to work with that person on a regular basis. Can you really focus on an inventory report being delivered by someone whom you've seen naked?

If you have to do it, though, there's nothing we can do to stop you. But keep these cardinal rules in mind: (1) Make sure they're not in the same reporting group as you. Many companies forbid you (officially or otherwise) from dating someone in your group. (1b) Make sure you don't report to them directly. Dating your boss may have worked in those old-fashioned romantic comedies, but today it's the quickest road to career suicide. (2) Be discreet. No hugging and kissing on the premises—even in the parking lot!—and no "Schmoopy" or "Snookums" at department meetings. (3) Make lunchtime about eating, and make an effort to maintain friendships with other coworkers. The last thing you want is to break up with someone and then, on top of your searing emotional pain, realize that you have no one to share a sandwich with.

TAKE CRITICISM GRACEFULLY

One of the toughest things about any job (let alone your first one) is learning how to deal with criticism. If you've been a student until now, you've had teachers critique and grade your work, but you haven't yet had to accept criticism from someone with direct influence over your future. You will inevitably screw up. Accept that now and you'll be a much happier person. Even if you manage to steer clear of major catastrophes, there will always be times when you're asked to alter your work and/or behavior. You just have to keep it all in perspective. Nobody's perfect, and being told that you need to improve something is not the end of the world.

When your supervisor tells you that you made a mistake, be open to it as a learning experience. Listen carefully and ask for guidance on how to fix the problem so that you don't repeat your error. If you get to the end of the conversation and you still don't understand what you need to do differently, ask. Neither you nor your boss wants to have this conversation again. It's awkward for him too.

Take ownership of your mistakes and accept responsibility for yourself; you'll earn your boss's respect that way. If someone didn't get you the necessary specs/figures/outfit in time, don't belabor the point or rattle off a list of excuses. Simply say, "I didn't have the order forms until 10 that morning, and even though I worked as quickly as I could I still missed the deadline." Then promise to do better next time—and follow through. If you've just taken a position as an assistant designer and were asked to offer up a few sketches and ideas, don't get all huffy if they're critiqued and not accepted. Learn why they weren't right and move on to the next assignment armed with some brand-new knowledge.

Dealing with Reviews

There are a lot of stories floating around HR departments these days about employees' parents calling to complain about their child's annual performance review. It's charming that your parents love and want to protect you, but if you're old enough to drink, you're old enough to take some heat. Here's the deal: Nobody likes receiving *or* giving these reviews, and half the time the paperwork gets dropped in a folder that collects cobwebs until the day you leave the company. Even if the process seems questionable and you resent your supervisor for offering criticism you disagree with, annual reviews are a workplace reality—not to mention a good opportunity for you to honestly evaluate your own performance.

Bosses realize that their entry-level employees are coming into the job raw. After all, they have to teach you *something*. An employee who can take direction positively and effectively is just as impressive as one who does flawless work from day one. So don't get mad if your boss says that you need to work on your communication skills, for example. You may be fuming to yourself, "Well, I'd communicate with my teammates a lot better if they weren't all *complete morons,*" but hold on for a second. Consider for a moment that you've been given an opportunity to improve yourself and your job skills. Maybe you could take a workshop on coping with difficult coworkers or start keeping emails in a "drafts" folder to allow yourself cool off for a day before shooting off angry messages in the heat of the moment. We all want to hear that we're doing a fabulous job, but that doesn't always happen. So if you get a bad (or just not-so-good) review, don't get mad—work on getting better.

Here are some tips on keeping your cool (and your perspective) during your review.

- **Know this going in: Your boss *has* to name an area where you can grow.** If your review came up 100 percent positive, the process would be totally meaningless. No matter what a star you are, everyone has something that they need to improve upon. Also keep in mind that part of your boss's job lies in building the company, so the improvement goals might be a result of your department's newly ambitious goals.

- **Don't take it personally, and don't focus on the negative.** So your boss thinks you have a poor sense of email etiquette and that you need to keep people in the loop better. That's not so bad. It's not like your supervisor told you that you're incompetent or anything. She's just giving your work persona a little (helpful) tweak. Keep it all in perspective.

- **If you do get slammed for something, pay attention.** Before you leave the review, make sure you know what's expected of you and what behavioral changes your boss wants (or needs) to see. If you're reprimanded for taking longer-than-appropriate lunch breaks, become a stickler for your schedule. Just don't overreact and stop eating altogether.

- **Focus only on your own review.** Don't worry about how John's or Jane's review is going, even if you have an opinion about their performance or feel that their poor work ethic has made it difficult for you to get your job done.

- **Don't blow your top on the spot.** If you find yourself losing your cool during the meeting, remember that you can always respond to a review with a brief, written response to human resources, making sure you forward a copy to your boss. If the feedback you receive is truly off base, it's okay to share your side of the story with specific examples of your contributions and accomplishments. But remember, a review is a necessary process in every company. So try to consider it a learning opportunity and not the ultimate judgment of your value as an employee.

- **Know your rights.** If your boss tells you that you're on probation and could be fired, figure out the exact nature of your company's termination policy. Employers are generally required to give you a written statement outlining the reasons for your probation, along with requests for improvement and a timeframe within which you need to accomplish the requested changes. Usually, an employee is given 90 days to improve before being fired. Your human resources department will be helpful if you're living in fear of being fired.

PREPARING FOR YOUR REVIEW

In the weeks leading up to your review, collect data on your own performance: What did you do? How much? How was it received? Designers should include the numbers of their designs that were manufactured and sold. PR assistant could tally attendance at press events or the number of client fashions that made the pages of *Us* magazine. Retail is very bottom line, so be prepared to show them the money. If you received a glowing note or even an email from a customer, vendor, coworker, or supplier, tuck it in the folder that you bring along to the review.

Chances are, you'll be given an opportunity to tell your supervisor what your goals are for the coming year, so do some thinking beforehand. Do you want to learn how to work a Gerber machine? Write more copy? Learn more about trend analysis? Part of the review process is demonstrating to the company that you remain interested and enthusiastic about your job.

Oh, and one last thing: Be on time.

TURNING DOWN A PROMOTION

Sometimes a boss, having seen how talented, creative, and all-around wonderful you are, will propose a change in your position that doesn't seem quite right for you. Not taking it can be tricky, but think carefully about what's best for you. Here are some red flags.

- **You have to relocate, but you have obligations in your current location.** Maybe you have an aging parent or significant other you'd like to be near, or you just invested in property.

- **The new job involves significantly different working conditions.** If you've been running a showroom and the company wants to put you on the road, consider how much you like driving, eating out, and sleeping in hotel rooms. Could you do it 20 weeks out of the year?

- **The timing is lousy.** A promotion usually means more responsibility. Are you in a position where you can spend more time and energy at work? We're not talking about whether you'll have to cancel your December trip to Cabo. If you have young children at home or are working toward a degree via correspondence courses, you may not be able to shoulder a load of new responsibilities.

If you do turn down a promotion or a lateral transfer, make sure the company knows how honored you were to be considered, and that you're happy with your current situation.

LEARN ON THE JOB

To enter some professions (medicine, law, or teaching, for example), you need to sign up for years of additional education. The fashion industry, however, operates differently. A good percentage of entry-level designers, PR neophytes, and those starting a retail career enter straight from their undergraduate work. But don't think that once you start full-time work you can just stop learning! Even though you won't have formal classes and assignments, you should still treat your first job as an opportunity to soak up all the information you can about your chosen field.

Seek a Mentor

You wouldn't want to go scuba diving without an experienced instructor, would you? And you wouldn't want to navigate the murky waters of the fashion industry without a veteran guide.

Most of the time your direct supervisor will serve as a mentor, but some larger companies have formal mentoring programs, in which someone from your team or a closely related department gets assigned to answer your questions about everything from where to get a cheap lunch in the area to understanding weekly sales reports. If you work in a large group setting and are looking for a formal mentor, ask your HR department (preferably the person who hired you) about getting hooked up with one.

If you're not getting enough feedback or explanation from your boss, look around the company for someone you can learn from informally. No need for a fancy commitment ceremony. If you go to a big meeting and see a friendly-looking senior employee give a smart presentation, write down her name. Look her up in the company directory and send her an email thanking her for her presentation. If she actually *is* friendly, then she'll write back and you'll have an opening to ask if she has any time to talk with you about the company, the fashion industry, or whatever it is you're itching to know. A simple approach like this can lead to coffee and then, hopefully, a casual work mentorship. You just have to take the first step.

Cozy Up to Your Colleagues

Your coworkers are a natural part of your network. Get to know them by striking up a conversation during break times. If you feel totally shy about it, start with someone on your team. Pay him a compliment, ask him a question about his work, or make a comment about something on his desk. You'd be amazed what can come from asking, "Is that a picture of your Chihuahua?" Coworkers can clue you into all kinds of important things that you'll never find out in your introductory HR session. They can tell you who to befriend in the office and who to avoid, as well as update you on any recent personnel dramas that might affect your work environment. If your immediate supervisor recently had a disastrous affair with the lead buyer and now throws a screaming fit when anyone mentions her name, a friendly tip from a coworker can spare you the indignity of having a computer monitor chucked at your head.

Remember that your colleagues also include other industry people who work outside your company. As soon as possible, get into professional organizations, such as Fashion Group International (fgi.org) or 24/7 Inc. (24seveninc.com), which sponsor networking events and career development panels. You can glean a lot of invaluable advice from these events—not to mention getting plenty of opportunities to make contacts across the industry. Your next mentor may come from an entirely different company! Be open to learning from anyone you meet.

66 Appearances mean a lot in fashion. There's favoritism in the workplace based on how you look—it's all about having great personal style and wearing the right labels. You want people to call you out on the hot outfit you're wearing and then be able to say, "Oh this? Thanks. It's Martin Margiela." You want to casually name drop hot labels whenever possible."

—**Erica Sewell,** former Fashion Designer; Assistant Director
Parsons Career Services

Study Up

Just because you're employed now doesn't mean you're done learning. You may not need to head back to school, but you do need to continue building a base of industry knowledge and keep your computer and technical skills up-to-date. Here are a few tips on how to stay competitive in the job market and informed for your current position.

- **Read everything you can get your hands on.** Figure out what your company keeps in its library. Many companies have subscriptions to major fashion industry periodicals that you can check out or read during your lunch break. If you can, get your own subscription to major publications like *Women's Wear Daily,* so you don't have to wait a week for an issue that shows up all shredded from the 20 people who read it before you. And pssst . . . don't forget: *WWD* posts job listings daily, so you can quietly keep your eye out for that next opportunity.

- **Utilize your company's educational opportunities.** Find out from human resources if your company offers on-site technology workshops or covers tuition for job-related classes—many do. If you work in the design department, brush up on your CAD skills on the company's dime. If you work in PR, take some classes in event planning. Colleges as diverse as Raritan Valley Community College in New Jersey, California State University–Fullerton, and George Washington University offer certificates in event planning. Beyond classes, check out seminars and conferences that relate to your field, and see if your company will cover your entrance fees and transportation costs.

- **Get connected to the industry.** Join a fashion organization to network and learn more about your field. Find out if your local fashion schools offer industry events for students that are also open to the public. Schools will often host panel discussions or have guest speakers present information on the job market, so subscribe to newsletters and events calendars from the design schools in your area.

In cities all around the country—and beyond—local fashionistas are organizing networking events through **fashion. meetup.com**.

THINK AHEAD

Chances are you'll have more than one job in your life. In fact, the average twentysomething can expect to have as many as five different *careers* before they retire. Your grandfather may have gotten a gold watch when he retired after 30 years on the job, but this ain't your grandfather's job market.

If you're serious about a career in fashion, part of your game plan should involve mapping out your next step. This is definitely a good topic to bring up with your mentor, assuming she isn't your direct boss. (Things could get ugly if your boss gets the idea you want to bolt, so tread carefully.) When it comes time to change companies or departments, you'll be glad you kept in touch with the people you work with, because as they move along in their careers they'll be valuable sources of information—not to mention recommendations.

When to Move

Unless someone wants you to do something illegal or immoral, plan on staying at your first job for at least a year or two. From a company standpoint, they spend about 18 months getting a new employee up to speed, so you may not get a great recommendation from them if you suddenly announce that you're leaving. If you like what you do and are learning from it, keep doing it, at least for a little while.

About those illegal and immoral issues

Here's a list of things employers should never ask you to do:

- Work under the table without filing taxes or reporting your income. Not only is it illegal, but it also hurts you in the long run because you don't contribute to your own Social Security account.

- Misrepresent the company or its products.

- See you socially one-on-one (like a date).

- Spend your own money on company business without reimbursement.

At some point, though, you'll probably get itchy and think seriously about leaving your job. Ask yourself the following questions before you waltz into your boss's office with a letter of resignation.

- **Have I learned everything I can at this job, in this position?** Hint: The answer is usually "no."

- **Have I participated in a whole year's worth of seasons?** If you haven't, potential employers might see you as flaky.

- **Is this a lateral move?** A lateral move involves taking a similarly titled job at another, similar company. Upward moves—which are far more desirable—can be promotions within your current company, more prestigious positions at a similar firm, or similar positions at a more prestigious firm. If you're thinking of making a lateral move, consider the fact that you'll still have to spend time getting used to your new company's politics and procedures, so it can often mean more of a setback than you might think. However, if you're currently working in menswear and you decide that your real calling lies in infant accessories, you may just have to suck it up.

- **What am I getting myself into?** See how well you can scope out the other job. Do the people there get along with one another? If you're replacing someone, why did he or she leave? Is it harder to get to the office/studio? Here's where your network comes in. Ask people you know if they know anyone at this new company, then call up your new second-degree friends to (delicately) get the inside scoop.

- **Am I leaving for the right reasons?** When you start a job you often can't predict what'll happen down the road in your personal life. Maybe you're getting married and moving to Boise. Maybe your family's business needs your help. Maybe you've finally accepted the fact that you hate New York/Los Angeles/Little Rock. Those are all sensible reasons for leaving a particular job. If you're leaving because the hours are long or because someone got mad at you, you're running from a job, which is very different than running toward something.

- **Is it a personality issue?** Even though you yourself are an angel and a model of sensible professionalism, sometimes there are people at your job you just can't stand to work with. If you've tried everything— being nice, asking for their help on a project, offering to help on one of theirs—it might be time to at least talk with your supervisor about switching departments or teams. If the problem is with your boss, don't blab all over that you're not getting along, but do seek wise counsel outside of work.

- **How does this move fit into my long-term career objectives?** Every time you think about switching jobs, the step ahead should improve your life in at least one of these three areas: what you do all day, where you do it, or who you do it with. If you're looking at a great opportunity that will open up even more opportunities down the line, go for it. If you don't have a clear sense of where the job might lead, carefully weigh the upsides and the downsides of both keeping and changing jobs. If you've spent a year as an executive trainee at Barney's and now know that you want to run your own hip, edgy boutique someday, you might be better off trying to land a job with Intermix, where you can learn more about your dream demographic. If, on the other hand, you have a feeling that luxury department stores aren't your thing but you haven't quite worked out what would suit you, consider staying put and gaining some more experience before you bolt.

8

EXPLORING RELATED OPPORTUNITIES

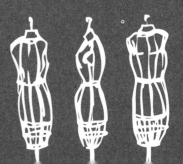

B y now you realize that the fashion world is pretty big. But in reality, it's even bigger than you might think. If you've got a passion for fashion but none of the career paths we've outlined appeal to you, you've still got plenty of other options. These jobs may not be the most obvious ones, but they're *all* essential in keeping the fashion world running.

FASHION MEDIA

If you've got fashion in your blood, chances are you've already spent a lot of time poring over magazines and analyzing photo spreads. The media plays a huge role in shaping the culture's trends and people's tastes, and it constantly needs a fresh supply of stylish people to make it all happen. *The Devil Wears Prada* didn't scare you off? Then read on to see if you have what it takes.

Top magazine publishing companies:

Hearst Corporation: *Harper's Bazaar; Cosmopolitan; O, The Oprah Magazine*

Condé Nast: *Vogue, Jane, Lucky*

Hachette Filipacchi: *Woman's Day, ELLE*

Fashion Magazines

Vogue, Allure, Lucky, ELLE . . . the list of great fashion magazines goes on and on. You probably already have your favorites, and you probably get a good workout carrying your stash of subscriptions from the mailbox to your comfy chair each month. You know your Diana Vreeland from your Carrie Donovan, that editorial content starts about two-thirds of the way through the magazine, and that you need to clear an entire weekend for those beautiful, fat September issues.

Check out any magazine masthead—that's the page at the front of the mag where all the staff members are listed—and you'll see that dozens of people work on any given issue. The three most fashion-forward classes are the editors, market editors, and the good folks in the art department.

EDITORS

Editors plan and generate a magazine's written content, which includes everything from short front-of-the-book pieces (calendar listings, gossip items, short book and entertainment reviews) to longer, in-depth features covering trends, news, and interviews. At a magazine like *ELLE* or *Vogue,* a number of acquiring editors handle various sections of the **book,** such as fashion (naturally), beauty, health and fitness, or features. At the larger magazines, each of those editors may be assigned an assistant or two. (Hint: That's where you come in.) The acquiring editors report to the managing editor, who in turn reports to the editor-in-chief. Both the managing editor and the editor-in-chief spend a lot of time in meetings, looking at the big picture and planning future issues. They don't have time to hold anyone's hand, so they rely on their editorial team to produce their respective sections on deadline, on budget, and on message.

book: Magazine speak for "magazine."

Editorial assistants are an important part of making that process run smoothly. On one hand, like assistants in any field, you'll do a lot of grunt work: filing, manning the phones, opening the mail, and getting the lunches. Plus, if you're working at one of the major magazines, you'll probably be living in a big city where your entry-level salary barely covers your rent, not to mention the fancy accessories you'll be tempted to buy to fit in with your city colleagues. On the other hand, most of your friends will think that you have an über-glamorous job, and you'll probably score a lot of free stuff from publicists eager to get their clients' products featured in your pages. And it won't all be busy work: Your assignments might also include fact-checking, proofreading, or writing short pieces called fillers. You may also help act as a liaison between the content providers—the freelancers or staff writers—and your supervising editors. As you gain both experience and your boss's trust, you'll get to start pitching your own ideas and take more responsibility for your section.

Most editorial assistants have degrees in journalism, communications, or English. No matter what you studied, you'll need solid writing and editing skills. You'll also need a thick skin—it can be hard to see your masterful article on the return of corsets massacred by your editor's red pencil. Not to mention the fact that magazines are notoriously hard to break into. You'll probably have to start by getting an internship (or three) or by writing short articles for free for small publications or websites. Once you've built up a file of clips (samples of your best writing), you'll have some ammunition to go after the job you want.

> **Freelance writing**
>
> Maybe you're a big *Sex and the City* fan and just *loved* the episode in which Carrie writes that article on handbags and then gets to go shopping in the legendary *Vogue* closet with Ron Rifkin. Slow your roll. It's not easy to have Carrie's life—it *is* TV, after all. (And frankly, in real life, Carrie probably couldn't have her life either. A closet full of Manolos on a writer's salary? Dream on!)
>
> If you want to try your hand at freelance writing, do not target *Vogue* on your first outing. You'll have to start small. Pitch your local newspaper, offering to cover Fashion Week, report on local boutiques, or discuss trends for the back-to-school season. You'll probably have to work for very little money at first to gain exposure, but every piece adds to your portfolio, and the more experience you gain, the better you'll be able to tell whether you've got the chops to make it. Mediabistro.com is a great place to learn more about freelancing for magazines and newspapers.

❝ The salary at the editorial assistant level is notoriously low. In addition, the environment can be catty, fiercely competitive, and demoralizing. You are a virtual extension of your supervising editor: fielding calls, dashing down to the mailroom and the coffee kiosk, faxing, filing, and emailing the whole day long.

But at the same time, you may be researching for a feature, testing a product, assisting with a photo shoot, brainstorming story ideas, and, with experience, beginning to write sidebars. Best of all, there's the perpetual thrill of seeing your efforts—no matter how small your contribution—combine with those of your coworkers on one tangible, glorious page. The only thing better than that is seeing your name in print."

—Anonymous, former Fashion Editorial Assistant

MARKET EDITORS

If your idea of a perfect Sunday is an afternoon spent poring through catalogs, you were born to be a market editor. Market editors are responsible for keeping tabs on all the new products and trends in a given area. They generally don't write or assign copy, although they do work closely with editors to plan pieces for the magazine. The market editor might notice, for example, that designers are increasingly using high-tech textiles for their everyday sportswear collections and suggest doing a feature on some of the most cutting-edge examples. The market editor would then work with another editor on creating the actual copy, while simultaneously pulling product examples to be featured in the accompanying photo spread.

Market editors usually have great personal style, often dressing to reflect the particular look of their magazine. Since so much of their work involves working with people—stylists, PR representatives, and designers, not to mention other magazine staffers—they need excellent people skills and a well-stocked Rolodex. All magazines operate on strict deadlines, so market editors, like the rest of their coworkers, need excellent organizational skills and an ability to multitask effectively. And, of course, they need a solid understanding of fashion history, so they can discern which trend cycles are really new and which are simply recycled.

As with most media jobs, internships are key. Multiple internships at various well-known magazines will set you up with the experience and contacts necessary to land a full-time job. Entry-level positions as market assistants involve tracking garments for photo shoots, keeping inventory for the fashion closet, and preparing items to be returned to designers' showrooms.

For more behind-the-scenes info, check out *Free Gift with Purchase,* a memoir by Jean Godfrey-June (beauty editor of *Lucky* magazine).

ART DEPARTMENT

Art side jobs at fashion mags include photo editors and graphic designers, all of whom report to the art director (usually a former graphic designer herself).

Photo editors assign, acquire, edit, and track the photography and images used in the magazine. They set up photo shoots, select photographers, negotiate fees, and make sure that everyone involved makes their deadlines. Drawing on their knowledge of photography, fashion, and style, photo editors strive to make images that are consistent with their magazine's specific visual needs. A photo editor at a fun, youthful magazine like *Seventeen,* for example, will need very different images from an edgier, more adult title like *W.* Photo editors need to be skilled photographers, even if they're not the ones actually taking the photos themselves.

They also need to be incredibly organized, since they're constantly working on multiple projects on tight deadlines. The good news is that you may be able to get into this field without a lot of formal education: A go-getter attitude and a strong work ethic, combined with knowledge of photographic equipment and processes, might just be enough to get you in the door for an internship.

Graphic designers make a magazine's look come together, incorporating all the visual elements from type to photos to illustrations into great-looking pages. These designers often work closely with a small team of three or four other designers. Important skills for this line of work include a background in art or design, computer skills (QuarkXPress, Illustrator, Photoshop, InDesign), an understanding of and facility with typography, and great creativity. A typical day might include tinkering with editorial layouts, attending status meetings, overseeing the flow of art coming into and going out of the art department, communicating with photographers/retouchers/agents, and overseeing the work of the art department interns. Graphic designers sometimes work with the advertising department on creating direct-mail pieces such as ads, postcards, email blasts, and promotional flyers. If you proceed all the way up to art director, you'll really get your hands on the book's visual elements, producing fashion shoots and working closely with both the creative director and your design team to execute stories.

Fashion Photography

It sure is a glamorous lifestyle, what with all the hanging around beautiful people and seeing your work in glossy magazines. But becoming a star fashion photographer can be as competitive as becoming a superstar model. Great photographers know how to do more than simply frame a beautiful shot. They need to be articulate and capable of explaining their concepts and inspiration. Networking is essential, since photographers must constantly seek out new faces, build teams of stylists and models they can call on a regular basis, and establish good relationships with assigning editors. They're responsible for managing all the logistic elements of a shoot, including overseeing assistants, getting the gear to the location, setting up lighting and camera equipment, directing models, and soothing nervous clients, art directors, and editors.

As with many freelance positions, fierce competition and the lack of a steady income can make some people queasy. Some photographers have agents who help them get work, while others negotiate directly with fashion houses, retailers, advertising agencies, or catalog retailers. Many aspiring fashion photographers work for little or no money when they start out, paying for photo shoots out of their own pockets and submitting the results to magazines in the hopes of landing a gig. Unseasoned photographers take this route to build a tear sheet (samples of published images) to legitimize their work and showcase their artistic vision.

If you'd rather work at the same location every day and dutifully pick up a paycheck twice a month, you might want to try the art department at a fashion magazine. But if you aspire to be the next Richard Avedon or Steven Meisel, try finding work as a photographer's assistant. You'll spend a lot of time running errands and schlepping around heavy photo equipment, but you'll also learn a ton. To land an assistant position, you'll need coursework in photography—including digital photography and darkroom experience—plus a portfolio of fashion projects. You should also know Photoshop or similar image software programs. If you're still in school, try working as a photographer for your student newspaper, magazine, or alumni office.

> 66 Fashion photography seems glamorous, but it isn't always! I was recently on the Lower East Side, shooting some models under a bridge, and I had to lie on the ground to get a shot. I ended up lying under the pipe that released water runoff, within inches of unidentifiable trash. I've also had to shoot out in the hot summer sun for over five hours, where I couldn't take a break or find shade because I had such a limited time to get the shoot done."
>
> —**Andrew Yee,** Fashion Photographer

Fashion Styling

Stylists help editors, art directors, and photographers come up with the right look for just about every media product imaginable, from TV shows to music videos to advertisements. They help select the models for a shoot, pick out clothing and accessories, determine makeup and

Find out more in *Breaking Into and Succeeding as a Fashion Photographer,* by Jennie S. Bev and Joshua Isard, or *An Autobiography,* by Richard Avedon.

hairstyles, and even help choose locations. As an assistant stylist, your job on the shoot might include pulling props and accessories, signing out and packing inventory, clearing items through security, ordering supplies, removing price tags from merchandise, pressing clothes, and keeping the prep room organized. And then, after the photo shoot wraps, guess what? You get to do it all in reverse. Assistant stylists need to be resourceful, extroverted self-promoters. You need to know just where to go to find that Bob Mackie gown for your boss's Cher-inspired shoot and then have the skills to negotiate a good price on the rental. Good stylists develop lots of contacts, so ditch your shyness and get ready to hustle for clients and build solid relationships with vendors.

Being a stylist is one of those cool jobs that everyone wants. Reality check: Opportunities are hard to come by, and the field is extremely competitive. There are limited opportunities to be had with major retailers, styling catalogs, and other promotional material, but the majority of jobs are freelance. Styling has no specific educational requirement, but experience in areas such as fashion merchandising, visual merchandising, or any visual arts field can help. Obviously, you should be up on current (and future) fashion trends and be able to pull together various influences into fresh, surprising combinations. The job can involve physical labor, since stylists have to set up props and sets. Can't find a red satin chaise for *Cosmopolitan*'s boudoir-inspired spread? Good thing you've got those carpentry skills (or know someone else who does).

To get into this field, you should definitely consider getting an internship or doing some volunteer work, such as assisting on film shoots in wardrobe coordination. You'll most likely start out working as a freelance assistant stylist and will almost always need to be in a major city like New York or L.A. to find steady work. You can try to get your foot in the door by finding a stylist whose work you like and then figuring out who their agent is. Pull together a slick-looking résumé and send it off to the agency, asking if your idol is looking for an assistant.

66 My top tips for aspiring stylists? Know your designers. Don't burn bridges. (Fashion is a small world.) And DON'T lose the clothing you've borrowed or mess it up at the shoot!"

—**Illya Knight,** Stylist

ALTERNATIVE DESIGN FIELDS

The people with the sketchbooks and the mannequins aren't the only folks who work in fashion design. If you've got a good eye, computer skills, or an uncanny sixth sense when it comes to color, you might just find your niche in one of the following fields.

CAD (Computer-Aided Design)

CAD artists work with fashion design teams to create computer-generated images of the team's garments, textile designs, and graphic elements. They produce clean versions of the designers' flat sketches and concept boards and help create seasonal presentation boards and **colorways.** When the team wants to change the colors of a garment—dialing down the intensity in a watermelon and acid green sundress, for example, to a softer mint and raspberry palette for fall—the CAD artists use programs like Photoshop to alter the original designs. After the CAD artist completes her work, the designers sign off on it and sample garments get produced. The CAD artist will often work with the assistant designers to ensure that images like logos and appliqués are correctly represented in samples. CAD artists must know how to create repeat patterns and understand various methods of textile printing and dying. They don't experience the same level of pressure as fashion designers, but things can get quite stressful due to the number of projects they work on simultaneously.

colorway: The palette of color options available for a given textile or garment.

These jobs require that you hit the ground running with excellent computer skills and a working knowledge of Photoshop, Illustrator, and U4ia. A bachelor's degree in fashion, textiles, or graphic design will prepare you the most, but an associate degree in a related field can get your foot in the door. You'll need the ability to draw and create images, but you don't have to have the speed or creative vision of an apparel designer. You'll need a portfolio of your work to get hired, and like any other designer, your samples should reflect your desired employers' aesthetic—show the team at Adidas your project for Roxy before you show them your work for Hello Kitty. If you're interested in learning more about this field, check out design schools that offer fashion-related CAD courses for the fashion industry.

Color Specialists

Large design companies have color teams. No, they don't all wear red one day and yellow the next. They research trends in color and work closely with the design team to develop the color palettes and color books for a given season. They create presentation boards, work with vendors to obtain materials in the correct shade, consult with merchandising teams on store displays, and even name and invent new colors. Color specialists know what colors sell best in each season. For example, they know that fall colors are always more muted than summer's, although the palette always has room for rich jewel tones as well. Entry-level color specialists use color-measuring spectrophotometers to compare the colors chosen by the team with lab dips (the fabric or yarn samples that come back from a dye house). Colorists need to be great team members and communicators, since they work with many groups, collaborating with sweater and woven design directors, dye houses and other vendors, and merchandisers.

Color work provides a great opportunity for a person without drawing skills to get involved in fashion design. In larger companies the work hours are fairly normal and the job responsibilities well-defined. As with most design-related fields, though, there are relatively few openings. Employers like to see design degrees, but you don't absolutely need one. To prepare for this field, develop your eye by taking classes in color theory and practicing mixing shades to match what you see in fabric, wallpaper, and paint. Most colorists start by working with *gouache,* a water-based color that mixes smoothly. You should have the ability to discern even the slightest variations in color. If you're interested in this field, become a member of myPANTONE, where you can read up on its free articles. Or you could try taking a class in color theory through your local college or art school's continuing education program.

Pantone, the company that develops the color books used by printers and other color specialists, creates seasonal color palettes and forecasts future trends through their Pantone Color Institute (pantone.com).

Costume Design

Costumes have a huge impact on our experience of a play, movie, or live performance. Just try to imagine *The Matrix* without Neo's black coat, Scarlet O'Hara without her curtain dress, or Darth Vader without his mask. Working in collaboration with the director, costume designers create the characters' basic looks before hiring a staff of costumers and wardrobers to carry out their plans. For some productions—say, science fiction films set in alien worlds—nearly every costume needs to be designed and produced from scratch. For productions set in more contemporary times, studios rely on their own wardrobe rooms to supply most of the costumes, and a staff of seamstresses and set costumers tailor the clothing to fit the actors.

Costume designers not only need to be well-organized and creative, they also need to be incredibly diplomatic since they have a lot of people to please—from the director who thinks the hero would look fierce in hot pink to the demanding ingénue who refuses to wear synthetic fabrics, everyone's got an opinion. You'll have to be a good listener but also a good negotiator who can articulate why you make the choices you do. Work environments can really vary, but one thing's for sure: The hours will be l-o-o-ong. A typical day can last over 10 hours, since you have to stay onset during filming in case anything goes wrong.

Although some costume designers majored in fashion, many studied theater and costume design at either the BA or MA level. Because the costume design industry is unionized, it can be hard to break into. A typical designer might start by working on college productions, move on to community theater, and then on to nonunion films before breaking into union productions. Beginning costume design assistants often work for free during the summers. For more information on costume design, visit the Costume Designers Guild, costumedesignersguild.com, or the Motion Pictures Costumers Guild, motionpicturecostumers.org. You should also pick up *Costume Construction*, by Katherine Evans-Strand, or *The Costume Book: The Non-Professional's Guide to Professional Results*, by Mary Burke Morris.

66 When I was working in the costume shop for the film *Superman*, I had to go to Fox and return Ben Affleck's red leather boots from *Daredevil*, which we'd been using for a sample. I found myself on a lot in Fox Studios late one afternoon on a holiday weekend, looking for the costume shop. There wasn't a soul to be found anywhere on the lot; all I found was a black cat running across my path. It was really eerie, but it was one of those moments that reminded me why I love costuming. I love being on studio lots, where at any moment you can be anywhere in the world—and it's only a great set designer's façade and a great costume designer's clothing."

—**Noelle Claire Raffy,** Costume Designer

"Rag pickers" are charged with digging around in wardrobe warehouses. Many entry-level assistants will spend hours finding boots for a crowded rodeo scene or enough costumes to outfit the crowd at a high-school graduation in 1970.

Apparel Graphics

From the company names that scream across T-shirts to the hibiscus flowers that dot Hawaiian-print swim trunks, the apparel industry deals with tons of graphics and images. Look a little closer and you'll realize that fashion graphic design extends to trims, packaging, logos (think of the Nike swoosh or the Lacoste alligator), brochures, presentations, and hang-tags. Graphic designers create signage for retail, work with print designers to develop advertising campaigns, and even develop graphics for shopping bags, key chains, and decals.

As an apparel graphics designer, you're driven by the same demands and deadlines as the design team. You're under tremendous pressure to create, correct, and deliver your designs so that they can be applied to the product on schedule. The graphics department services everyone from the design team to the production people, and they've all got differing opinions you have to consider. To succeed in this job you must be able to take constructive criticism. If a client or department leader doesn't like the colors you've used in a brochure, you have to either adjust your work accordingly or be able to politely explain why lime green really does capture the spirit of the spring line.

Graphic design is a wide field, with a steady demand for designers who can apply graphics to clothing and accessories. Positions are available for both full-time staff designers as well as freelancers. Most apparel graphic designers have training in either graphic design or fashion design. To land a job in this field, you'll need a great portfolio that demonstrates your superb drawing skills as well as your ability to design to the fashion industry's needs. It should include examples of logo design, designs for apparel (T-shirts in particular), hangtags, and brochures. Excellent computer skills in Photoshop and Illustrator are essential, as is an understanding of printing and production processes. You'll be a stronger candidate if you know typography, silk-screening, and how to create repeat patterns. With experience, graphic designers can become art directors and creative directors.

Makeup Design

On the runway, in photo shoots, onstage, and onscreen, makeup artists create the faces that go with the fashions. If you've got an eye for color and a deft hand, makeup design provides a great opportunity to participate creatively in fashion. Being a makeup artist can involve crazy hours, insanely early call times, and—since you'll usually be hired on a freelance basis—an uncertain pay schedule. At the beginning, you'll have to learn how to live on a salary that's only slightly ahead of minimum wage. But the perks include tons of free hair and makeup products, professional discounts on cosmetics, and plenty of celebrity sightings, not to mention a satisfying, creative career. Because so much of the work takes place in high-stress situations, you'll often find yourself soothing skittish models and defusing diva blow-ups to maintain a friendly, easygoing work environment. You'll also need to be able to take direction from art directors, designers, and photographers. If the designer says he wants the girls to look fresh, young, and J. Crew all-natural, for example, you better not send Gisele out on the runway looking like Cleopatra.

Since most makeup artists work on a freelance basis and each client pays different rates, you need to be a good business person to negotiate good deals for yourself. Required training varies, but working at a department store cosmetics shop or a stand-alone shop like MAC can be a smart way to get your feet wet. You can also take classes at cosmetology schools, where you can learn all about the art and science of makeup application. The truth is, most makeup artists are largely self-taught. If you're serious about makeup design you'll eventually need to develop a portfolio that showcases your style, your versatility, and how well your work translates onto the printed page. Make sure to work with a good fashion photographer who can accurately capture your designs. Makeup artists also create comp cards, postcard-size self-promotion pieces that show one to four photos of their work, as well as personal websites with a digital version of their design portfolio.

Visit the American Association of Cosmetology Schools at beautyschools.org.

Need a role model?

Read up on these makeup superstars: Pat McGrath (currently developing lines for Cover Girl and Armani), Dick Page (Prescriptives), Jeannine Lobell (founder of Stila), and Bobbi Brown. For more inspiration, check out the MAC website (maccosmetics.com) for profiles on several of their professional makeup artists. Or pick up the late, great Kevyn Aucoin's fabulous books on makeup effects: *The Art of Makeup* (1996), *Making Faces* (1999), and *Face Forward* (2001).

Fashion Design for Dolls

Dolls—and especially the clothes they wear—are big, big business. In 2004 alone, American Girl grossed $379 million in sales. At the major doll companies, such as Mattel, American Girl, and MGA (makers of Bratz), designers create everything from nurses' uniforms to bathing suits to sequined evening gowns. Doll designers work in teams to oversee all elements of the product, so besides the outfits themselves, they also produce accessories, packaging, and matching outfits for companion dolls. Fashion teams are often housed in the same building as the company's other designers, and the work environment is both more corporate than at small fashion companies and more casual than at the big fashion houses. The hours tend to be shorter and more predictable than those of designers in the apparel world. Beware, though: The pressure just before Toy Fair in January ratchets up just as intensely as it does before Fashion Week. It can be a real thrill to see your designs lining the aisles at toy stores and getting snapped up during the holiday rush. Keep in mind, though, that you might find it hard to transition into full-size fashion once you've established yourself in this niche field.

Like any designer, you'll need to understand your customer. Seven-year-old toy fans and twentysomething fashionistas want very different things, after all. You'll need strong sketching and computer skills to present your concepts. You'll also need solid communication skills, since you'll have to pitch your ideas in team meetings and work closely with team leaders and production departments (often located overseas). It's not uncommon to have to implement six or seven corrections to a concept in a single day, so you'll need to be calm and flexible. Many designers for doll fashions have degrees in full-size fashion design. Some have degrees in toy design, currently offered at only a few colleges nationwide. Toy design programs provide courses in fabrication and sketching as well as child psychology and play patterns. For more information, visit Women in Toys (womenintoys.com) or the Toy Industry Association (toy-tia.org).

FASHION BUSINESS

Visual merchandising, trend forecasting, and human resources are career paths that offer the fashion-obsessed other outlets for their creativity and people skills. If you've ever wondered what it would be like to be the person who plans the gorgeous window displays at Anthropologie, or you would *die* to get paid to think about trends all day, check out these career options.

Visual Merchandising

Think about your favorite stores—the ones whose elaborate window displays and inviting layouts always manage to draw you in and make you spend the last crumbs of your hard-earned paycheck. A visual merchandiser was responsible for creating that enticing environment. Visual merchandisers design the atmosphere of a store, developing displays and decorating schemes that bring in, drive them to buy more products, and reinforce the brand's image. Most visual merchandisers work in-house, but there are some freelance jobs available. In-house visual merchandisers also create displays for trade shows, aimed at getting professional buyers to purchase their company's line. The best thing about visual merchandising lies in the wide variety of tasks. On any given day you might find yourself designing lighting schemes, choosing paint colors, and designing props. It can be hard, though, to keep those shopping environments fresh after you've been designing them for a while—after all, how many new heart-themed displays can you come up with every Valentine's Day?

Visual merchandisers come from a variety of backgrounds, including interior design, architecture, consumer psychology, graphic design, fashion merchandising, and fine arts. Coursework in merchandising is a must, and experience working in a retail store will help you understand what makes customers tick. You'll also have to demonstrate an ability to collaborate with others, because this job involves working closely with sales staff, buyers, and store managers. If you don't like getting your hands dirty or you like coming up with ideas but can't be bothered with the technical work involved in bringing those ideas to life, visual merchandising may not be a good fit for you. To see if you might enjoy this career path, try getting a part-time job or internship assisting a visual merchandiser. If you're studying fashion design, you might approach a retail store and ask if you could help with their displays while working as a salesperson. Salaries for visual merchandisers generally range from $20,000 to $50,000 but can go much higher depending on the brand and the merchandiser's level of experience.

Fashion and Trend Forecasters

Are you a notorious fashion dictator? Do you roll your eyes when you see girls in last season's hippie boho skirts? Did you know you could get paid for doing that? It's true: There are companies out there that spend all their time telling other companies what's cool (or not). Teams of trend-spotters, photographers, researchers, and analysts continually travel to New York, London, Paris, and Milan—the four fashion capitals—to research buzzworthy fabrics, colors, stores, trends, and designers. These forecasting companies then create detailed reports that companies purchase and study before designing a new line. Fashion retailers will often have a major trend company such as Worth Global Style Network or Fashion Snoops make a presentation at their annual sales meeting. Sometimes larger fashion companies employ their own in-house forecasting teams.

Fashion forecasters need a wide skill set. Naturally, you'll need to have an eye for color and a sixth sense for fashion: When looking at a huge rack of presale clothes, forecasters can zero in on which garments will prove the hottest sellers and which will spark huge campus trends. In addition, you'll need to know how to read statistical reports and how to communicate effectively, both visually and verbally. Knowledge of graphic design programs such as Photoshop, Illustrator, and Quark will allow you to create beautiful presentations of the images you've collected on your trips. Courses like art history and interior design will help you understand the relationship between current fashion and historical trends—not to mention training you to see how a beautiful vintage upholstery textile might look amazing when fashioned into an evening jacket. Travel experience and a facility with foreign languages look great on a résumé. Forecasting is a small field with relatively few openings, but if you land a job you can earn a pretty solid living—these positions can pay from $50,000 a year to over $100,000 with experience. For more research on large trend companies, check out Worth Global Styling Network (wgsn.com) and Cotton Incorporated (cottoninc.com).

Start your own "cool file." Clip out pictures of fashions, furniture, shapes, colors, and anything else that catches your eye. Label each piece, including where and when you found it: "Cotton floral print, Hawaii, April 2007 vacation."

66 One trend that we anticipated through our research at ESP Trendlab was the recent grunge resurgence. We saw chunky, layered knits and combat boots emerging on the street and runway long before the trend really caught on. The chaos of the world political situation was leading people to cocoon themselves and focus on self-nurturing. People wanted simplicity and beautiful but comfortable fabrics, not the bling and label/logo consciousness that seemed so appealing just a few years prior. So keeping abreast of what's happening politically and socially is a big part of understanding the future of fashion and is essential in trend forecasting."

—**Angela Ringo,** Research and Production
ESP Trendlab

Human Resources and Recruiting

Human resources professionals manage a company's employee-related matters, such as staff recruiting and training, performance appraisal, and salary and benefits issues. In small companies, the HR person might also serve as the accountant, office manager, or even the owner. In-house recruiters and researchers come from all backgrounds, from fashion design to English lit. Some HR professionals, especially recruiters and trainers, come from the retail world, having excelled at developing teams of great salespeople in their stores.

Several recruiting agencies focus specifically on finding capable employees for clients in the fashion industry. These professionals spend time talking with potential candidates about open positions, reviewing portfolios, and recommending candidates to their clients. Recruiters also serve as counselors for jobseekers, advising them on everything from how to spin their summer in Bali as relevant career experience to appropriate interview clothing.

Entry-level human resources employees usually provide a lot of administrative support. They post ads, collect résumés, arrange interviews, and keep the files in order. Many colleges now offer a degree in human resources, but it's usually possible to enter the HR field with a liberal studies degree and some retail management experience. Great organization and communication skills are a must. If you're thinking of going into recruiting, you'll need to demonstrate an ability to work with others and be "on" and extroverted when necessary. You have to be comfortable with reaching out to strangers and quickly establishing a rapport. Awareness of the fashion industry and an ability to insightfully review design portfolios are also essential. Recruiters often report high levels of stress, as companies may demand that a minimum number of jobs be filled on a regular basis. HR salaries range from $40,000 to $100,000+, and recruiting firms often pay commissions based on placements.

9

STARTING YOUR OWN FASHION BUSINESS

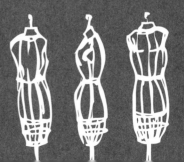

Most people go into fashion hoping to be anointed the next big thing. But the truth is that very few designers successfully open their own businesses, and those who do almost all got their feet wet by working for someone else first. Starting your own business is, well, serious business. Anyone currently running one will tell you that it's not as easy as it looks, and most pros will tell you to work in the industry for a few years before jumping into your own line. While everyone knows the stories of freshly graduated design students making huge splashes on the scene (paging Proenza Schouler), those experiences are definitely the exception to the rule. If you're still determined, though, read on for tips and advice.

DECIDE IF YOU HAVE WHAT IT TAKES

Starting your own line takes more than talent. If you're serious about starting your own line, tomorrow or in a few years, here are a few things that you'll absolutely need to succeed.

- **Lots of money:** You probably realize that you'll need money for material and equipment. But you'll also need money for lawyers and accountants and to pay sample-makers and manufacturers, hire public relations help and create media kits, pay employees, get insurance, buy a business license, rent a work space, and a million other things that go along with running a business. The amount of money that it realistically takes to launch a business—which can be anywhere from tens of thousands to $100,000 or more—can be prohibitive for anyone whose last name isn't Hilton.

- **Total commitment:** Owning your own business means thinking about your business 24/7, plus full responsibility for everything. No downtime, no vacation, no sick days. You could be running a fever of 105 and still find yourself in the office, yelling at your factory representative over the phone for losing your fall collection, dealing with a fleet of broken sewing machines, staring at a pile of unprocessed invoices and an unbalanced account ledger . . . Did we mention you won't have a life? And whatever happened to actually, you know, designing?

- **Experience:** Most successful designers started out assisting others to gain experience. Working as an assistant designer, especially in a small company, allows you to observe how the pros manage their day-to-day business, work with vendors, build relationships, handle crises, and create marketing and sales plans for their product. Young, untested designers often make basic business mistakes such as starting off with insufficient capital and too few industry contacts. You need advisors to guide you through the tough spots, plus hands-on experience so you can anticipate (and deal with) the myriad problems that can arise on a daily basis.

- **Business sense:** Most fashion entrepreneurs dream of having their own lines so that they can spend their days creating beautiful garments. But once your name's on the door, you have to split your attention between designing the clothes and running the business end—whether you're a one-man band working at your dining-room table (don't worry; you'll be too busy to eat there anyway) or you've got a dozen employees and window displays at Barney's. You have to understand and take responsibility for your company's financial health, even if you end up hiring an accountant to manage all the complicated stuff. You'll be your own quality-control officer, purchasing agent, shipping clerk, and salesperson. You'll handle all bank transactions and you'll read contracts and legal documents like your life depended on it.

- **Excellent people skills:** When you run your own business, you are the public face of your company. You need to build a reputation and network aggressively with fellow designers, investors, and the media. If you can barely approach strangers at a party or have a hard time articulating what you want, you could be in trouble. No matter how talented a designer you are, you'll constantly have to rely on other people to get

Always be ready.
You never know when you'll meet a potential investor in a random place. Be able to explain what makes your product unique in 30 seconds or less.

your product completed, on the market, and into consumers' shopping bags, so good business relationships are critical to your success.

- **Great communication skills:** No one's going to articulate your thoughts for you or keep track of your paperwork. You need to be your own secretary. Learn to concentrate on one conversation at a time— don't answer the other line, your cell phone, or your email. Listen more than you talk. Always repeat what the other person says to make sure you heard it correctly. Get information in writing. Ask for what you want, in detail. Tell the truth. Return every phone call and every email within 24 hours. Don't whine. Thank people for a job well done.

Learn from the masters

Almost every famous designer you can think of did his or her time working for (and learning from) someone else. Here are just a few examples of the fashion stars who apprenticed with other designers before branching out on their own:

Donna Karan worked at Anne Klein for almost 15 years before launching DKNY.

Narciso Rodriguez designed for Calvin Klein after working at Anne Klein (under Donna Karan!).

Peter Som worked for Calvin Klein and Michael Kors.

Isaac Mizrahi worked at Calvin Klein and Perry Ellis.

Benhaz Sarafpour designed for Anne Klein, where she worked alongside Narciso Rodriguez, as well as Isaac Mizrahi.

Proenza Schouler designers Lazaro Hernandez and Jack McCollough interned at Michael Kors and Marc Jacobs.

Doo-Ri Chung worked with Donna Karan while still in school and then at Geoffrey Beene for several years as lead designer.

Tracy Reese worked as Martine Sitbon's design assistant and later as design director for Perry Ellis before successfully launching her own line.

Zac Posen interned at Nicole Miller before becoming design assistant at Tocca.

---

66 Unless you're a young star who is immediately picked up by a large luxury group, the best way to gain experience is to work for another company or designer. This will give you a taste of the business and an understanding of the process. If you do break out on your own, don't limit yourself to the high end of fashion. The luxury market is a very small component of the garment business, and there is a lot more room in the casual market. Pursue all the options. Take risks and be adaptable.

—Lexy Funk, President and Founder
Brooklyn Industries

DEVELOP A BUSINESS PLAN

Businesses aren't born, they're built. If you're serious about starting a line of your own, you'll want to think carefully about creating a **business plan,** a document that describes your product and target customer as well as your strategy for designing, manufacturing, marketing, and selling your product. Here are the eight basic things you need when setting up your plan.

1. **Money:** The truth is simple. When new businesses fail, it's usually because they don't have enough money. Know how much money you're going to need and how you're going to get it and include this fiscal outline in your business plan. Depending on what kind of line you're starting, costs can range from around $10,000 (if you're working from home and don't need to make any income for a year or so) to over $100,000 if you expect your hot-hot-hot product to sell about 10,000 units. Where to get the money? Most startup companies are funded through the business owner's own investments (personals savings or a loan against their homes) or through a loan with the Small Business Administration. You might also think about seeking outside investors—preferably ones who didn't give birth to you. You can try to defray your initial costs by cutting deals with your suppliers or taking pre-orders to fund your first production run.

2. **A clearly defined product:** Think about what makes your designs or brand unique. You'll need a strong answer to pitch your company to potential investors or vendors. Are you doing sportswear or eveningwear? Menswear or womenswear? Is your aesthetic hip and urban or elegant and retro? Maybe your fabrics are unique, or you're using old-school hand-tailoring, or you're combining materials than aren't usually seen in this market. Whatever it is, it had better be compelling.

66 I wanted to do a vintage-inspired pin-up girl line, kind of Bettie Page meets June Cleaver: very tarty, but sexy, with luxurious fabrics. I wanted the line to have a sense of humor to it. I also carved out a niche for myself with my fabrics. No one was using prints when I first started, so I stuck to classic prints like polka dots, cherries, and always leopard! Loungewear Betty became this character I created, who's really a much more fabulous version of myself."

—**Monnie McCleary,** Founder and Designer
Loungewear Betty

3. **A clearly defined customer:** Fashion is dictated by the customer. Who's going to buy your product? Articulate your target customer's age, financial means, and style. Also think about the fashion role models or aspirations of your target customer. Would Kimora Lee Simmons represent a typical customer/person who'd wear your clothes or are you going for understated elegance, say a look embodied by Gwyneth Paltrow?

4. **Clearly defined competition:** You'll need to think about what's already out there in the market and how you're going to distinguish your product. Why does the world need another line of polos with a reptile logo? Maybe yours is an iguana logo and your line skews urban punk with a twist of preppy. If the market seems to be saturated with something similar to your product, you'll need to spin why your line will stand out from the crowd.

5. **Legal status:** If you're serious about starting a viable business, you can't just start selling your stuff out of the trunk of your car. You need to set up your business as a legal entity so that your company

can grow and—just as important—so you can protect your personal assets. Consult a lawyer and an accountant first, and be ready to talk to them about your five-year plan. They'll be able to advise you as to what business structure you should adopt. Here are a few of the most common ways to make it legal.

» *Sole proprietorship*
In a sole proprietorship, you are responsible (and liable) for all financial matters. Many designers start out this way because it's easy and cheap, but the problem with a sole proprietorship is that your assets aren't shielded if something goes wrong. If someone falls down and breaks a leg in your studio, you'll likely get stuck paying their medical bills.

» *Partnership*
You and a partner are jointly responsible for all financial and legal matters. As with a sole proprietorship, your personal assets aren't shielded. If 20 years down the line an old vendor comes looking for an overdue payment, you and your partner will be held personally accountable for those debts. Because of this, partnerships and sole proprietorships are usually not recommended for young designers just starting out. Plus, in a partnership, disagreements or miscommunications between partners can be costly. If your partner signs a deal with a new manufacturer and doesn't run it by you, it'll be your tough luck if their business goes under while you were anticipating a big order from Saks.

» *Corporation*
This is a highly structured business format, which requires a state license, a board of directors, annual meetings and minute-keeping, and the issuing of stocks. Unlike the first two business models, corporations come with a certain financial peace of mind, since you cannot be held personally responsible for any debts incurred by your company. There are two types of corporations: an S corporation for smaller operations and a C corporation for bigger businesses.

» *Limited Liability Company*, or *LLC*

LLCs are a little like proprietorships and partnerships and a little like corporations. An LLC offers you more flexibility than a corporation but comes with the same financial protection. Another advantage of an LLC is that you can separate voting rights from share ownership, so that you maintain creative control of your company even when another party has more money invested in it than you do. One hassle about operating an LLC is that in states like New York you are required to make public announcements whenever you do things like initially form your company. These types of ads can run $1,500 or more in major publications like *WWD*.

6. **Lawyers and accountants:** If you've still got a mountain of student debt to pay off, the idea of hiring lawyers and accountants might seem ludicrous to you. But trust us: You'll be glad you got some professional advice. You don't have to have a full-time accountant on staff, but you should consult one about managing your taxes and tracking your expenses. Get a lawyer involved sooner rather than later to advise you about creating a legal business and to help you file the appropriate papers, ensure that your company name is available for use, and discuss other legal issues such as trademarks.

❝❝I wasn't prepared for the legal battles. I had designed what people know as the 'scrunchy' a year before it existed, then was legally pursued by a major hair accessories company for years because they thought my product was too similar to theirs—I had to spend a lot of money defending myself. Then there was the crooked businessman who said he'd get me incorporated. Later, I found out that instead of filing an application for a new corporation under my name, he just renamed one of his inactive companies 'Colette Malouf,' which meant that all of a sudden he owned my name. It was very stressful, and it all happened my first few years in business. I'm glad those days are over!"

—Colette Malouf, Jewelry and Accessory Designer

7. **Marketing plan:** You'll probably need to get some expert assistance here. Find out how much product is sold every year in your niche (hand-knit scarves and hats, baby clothes, embroidered T-shirts) and then estimate how much of that market you could conceivably acquire. If you think that you can assume 1 percent of the national market, make sure you have the capacity to produce that much. Be careful, too, if your item is seasonal—there's a big push for holiday items during July (to show at the gift shows on both coasts) but not much of a market for these cozy accessories in May.

8. **Sales plan:** You'll need to determine how much your product will sell for, where it'll sell, and how much it'll sell annually. You'll also need to consider how you'll promote your product. If you're going to sell funky, young designs reminiscent of Ella Moss, you might choose a similar sales plan, pricing your dresses in the $110 to $150 range and selling them in small boutiques like Olive and Bette's and select department stores such as Barney's Co-op. You also have to decide whether you'll serve as your own sales rep or hire an outside agent. Experienced sales reps have established customer bases and often represent several independent designers, taking a commission on all the sales they deliver.

For more information on business plans, visit *Inc.* magazine's Start-Up Business Center at inc.com/resources/startup.

STUDY UP

If all the hard work and heartache hasn't scared you yet, learn more about launching your own business with the following recommended resources.

- ***The Fashion Designer Survival Guide,*** by Mary Gehlhar
  This is a great book on how to set up a fashion business with your eyes wide open. Gehlhar is the fashion division director for Gen Art (genart.org), an organization that assists young designers in getting their work shown and starting their own lines.

- **Global Purchasing Group,** globalfashionbuys.com
  This buying office in New York purchases for retailers throughout the

Zac Posen showed a collection in Gen Art's 2001 show that put him on the map.

United States and actively seeks work from young fashion designers. They also offer workshops and classes on production management.

- **Fashion Business, Inc.,** fashionbizinc.org
  A fashion incubator on the West Coast, FBI offers seminars and classes on various aspects of the apparel industry. They have resources and networking opportunities that introduce new and small-business owners to consultants specific to their company's needs.

- *Fashion for Profit,* by Frances Harder, fashionforprofit.com
  Harder, a designer, businesswoman, and the founder of Fashion Business Inc., offers a detailed guide to creating and marketing your own line. You can also buy a "business starter package" that includes Harder's *Forms for Profit* and *Costing for Profit,* plus a CD/DVD of a fashion business seminar led by Harder and several other industry pros.

- **The Market NYC,** themarketnyc.com
  At this fashion market located in the Nolita neighborhood of Manhattan, designers can buy booth space on the weekends and sell their wares directly to the public. Many designers whose work can be seen in national magazines such as *Lucky* and *In Style* sell their garments here. The low overhead costs mean that designers without enough money for their own shops or commissions to larger stores can still get great retail exposure.

- **The Alexander Report,** thealexanderreport.com
  A great B2B site, this online directory can help you find all kinds of services, resources, and vendors and is especially helpful if you're still building your contact list. The site claims to help you "find what you're looking for . . . from where to get scissors to which companies sell silk brocade, to where to get a visa for overseas travel."

- **My Own Business,** myownbusiness.org
  This website offers free online courses in running your own business. Includes a guide to writing a business plan, a list of recommended books, and a directory of other business resource websites.

- **Small Business Administration,** sba.gov

  A key partner for many startup companies, the SBA offers seminars on starting a business, recordkeeping, copyright information, and funding. Use the website to find your local SBA center and learn about available services in your area. They also offer free online courses and e-books.

- **Creative Capital,** creative-capital.org

  This nonprofit organization in New York offers short- and long-format workshops for artists and entrepreneurs.

- **Jeffrey Fox's books on business**

  A classic series of business books from a marketing maven. Check out *How to Become a Rainmaker, How to Become a Marketing Superstar,* and *How to Make Big Money in Your Own Small Business.*

- **The Chamber of Commerce,** uschamber.com/chambers/directory

  Consider joining—or at least visiting—your local Chamber of Commerce and getting to know the other individual business owners in your community. They can provide support, professional friendship, and maybe even business leads!

- **SCORE,** www.score.org

  SCORE Provides resources and expertise to maximize the success of existing and emerging small businesses. An all-volunteer organization of retired executives, they even provide online business counseling.

PART III: CAREER-PLANNING TOOLS

FURTHER RESOURCES

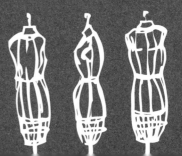

INDUSTRY NEWS AND INFORMATION

- **Accessories Magazine,** accessoriesmagazine.com
  Provides extensive information on trends, news, and trade shows
  for all types of accessories, from handbags and hats to watches and
  jewelry.

- **BusinessWeek.com**
  A great website for doing research on any type of business. There's a
  section called "Innovation and Design" that's terrific for reading up on
  what's hot in the fashion world and a section with news and resources
  for starting small businesses.

These starred (*) resources are some of our favorites.

- *California Apparel News,* apparelnews.net*
  Weekly trade publication covering the business of the fashion
  industry, focusing on the West Coast. If you don't live in Los Angeles,
  you can subscribe online. A chief resource for L.A.-based fashion
  industry want ads.

- *Career Opportunities in the Fashion Industry,* by Peter Vogt,
  Checkmark Books, 2002
  Gives a broad overview of the various career paths available in fashion
  and offers general salary ranges for entry-level to senior positions.

- *Daily News Record,* dnrnews.com*
  Weekly industry paper that covers menswear news and trends. The
  website includes an online job board.

- **Fashion Net,** fashion.net
  Chic website, great for viewing fashion show photos and reading up on
  different labels. Has a guide to the "green" fashion companies, which
  have environmentally friendly and socially responsible policies.

- **Fashion Wire Daily,** fashionwiredaily.com
  Newswire service devoted to fashion, celebrity style, and
  entertainment news.

- **firstVIEW,** firstview.com
  Posts photos of runway shows in New Delhi, Moscow, Kuala Lumpur, and many other cities around the world. Track trends as they move across the globe!

- *Forbes,* forbes.com
  A great resource for learning about specific companies. Type *fashion* into the website's search menu to find numerous articles about the financial end of the apparel industry.

- *Footwear News,* footwearnews.com
  E-zine covering footwear news, trends, major players, and business strategies. Includes comprehensive calendar of events in the shoe industry.

- **Hoover's,** hoovers.com*
  An excellent, comprehensive source of information on public companies. Free info includes company overview, leadership, dollar volume in sales, and key competitors. Extensive reports available for a fee.

- *The New York Times,* nytimes.com*
  Great resource for stories on current fashions. The Thursday and Sunday Styles sections are especially informative.

- **The Style Council,** stylecouncil.com
  Design studio that offers trend forecasting for men's, women's, and children's textiles. You can get a free peek at their trend reports online, including Pantone color IDs.

- **Style.com***
  Online home of Condé Nast's fashion bibles, *Vogue* and *W* magazine. Scope out the latest runway shows and get industry buzz on the hottest designers. Make sure to check out British *Vogue* too, at vogue.co.uk; some stylists and designers think it's the best fashion site out there for cutting-edge fashion news. Menswear gets its day in the sun at men.style.com, the website of Condé's men's mags, *GQ* and *Details*.

Style leaders to keep tabs on:

Allure
ELLE
Esquire
Harper's Bazaar
GQ
In Style
Lucky
Marie Claire
Nylon
Paper
Seventeen
Surface
Visionaire
Vogue
W

- **_Women's Wear Daily (WWD),_** wwd.com*
  New York–based newspaper covering the fashion business; a daily must-read for anyone and everyone in the industry. Includes comprehensive job listings. _WWD_ also prints regional editions in Los Angeles, Atlanta, Dallas, and Chicago.

Fashion blogs and chatrooms

thefashionspot.com/forums/chat.php
Join conversations about designers, models, careers, and trends. Free registration.

fashioncapital.co.uk
British site with discussions on sourcing and the business end of the fashion industry. Even if you're U.S.-based, many of the issues and concerns are the same.

boards.core77.com
Free exchange and discussion of design-related ideas. Topics include Students 'n' Schools, Design Employment, and Design in Asia.

apparelsearch.com
Discussion groups on machinery, closeouts, employment, and classifieds, plus a directory of fashion blogs.

nymag.com/fashion/blog
Runway talk, fashion week diary, party report, and links to more blogs.

PROFESSIONAL ORGANIZATIONS

- **7th on Sixth,** 7thonsixth.com
  An organization founded in the early '90s to give American fashion collections a platform and to help them gain global exposure. 7th on Sixth produces Olympus Fashion Week in New York and Mercedes-Benz Fashion Week in Los Angeles. They also publish the _Daily Front Row,_ a magazine for industry insiders and the media.

- **Accessories Council,** accessoriescouncil.org
  Nonprofit trade association that works to increase consumers' use and awareness of accessories.

- **Council of Fashion Designers,** www.cfda.com
  Nonprofit trade organization of top fashion and accessories designers. The annual CFDA fashion awards are considered one of the fashion industry's top accolades. The organization offers scholarships and special apprenticeships to emerging fashion designers.

- **Fashion Group International,** fgi.org*
  Nonprofit organization that serves the fashion, accessories, beauty, and home design industries. FGI provides excellent networking opportunities, although membership is usually limited to professionals with a few years of experience.

- **Gen Art,** genart.org*
  Nonprofit organization that supports emerging artists, musicians, filmmakers, and designers. Gen Art helps showcase the work of young fashion designers and sponsors fashion shows, exhibitions, and competitions.

RECRUITERS AND JOB LISTINGS

- **24seventalent.com***
  Great resource for those seeking jobs in the fashion industry. Sponsored by 24seven Inc., a bicoastal search agency specializing in placing fashion and graphic designers in freelance and full-time positions.

- **Craigslist,** newyork.craigslist.org, losangeles.craigslist.org, etc.
  Looking for a job, an apartment, and an auto mechanic in the same city? Try Craigslist, the nation's bulletin board. Pick your city, then cruise the job section.

Note: We don't necessarily endorse all the job-hunting resources listed here. Different people will have different experiences with different recruiters—it all depends on the individual person you're working with, what kinds of jobs are currently available, and what kind of background you have.

FURTHER RESOURCES

235

- **Fashion Net,** www.fashion.net/jobs
  A popular collection of job listings, from the chic fashion webzine.

- **The Fashion Tool,** thefashiontool.net
  Job listings site designed by HR experts. Offers exclusive access for paid members.

- **Fashion Windows,** www.fashionwindows.com
  Provides fashion industry news as well as job postings. Access to much of the site requires registration and a monthly fee.

- **Infomat,** infomat.com/career
  The career section of this fashion search engine lists their top 25 employment websites, with detailed information and ratings on each.

- **Project Solvers,** project-solvers.com
  New York–based freelance and full-time placement service, with a great fashion resource section. If you're not sure you want to work in NYC, look here for a freelance gig so you can try it out without a huge commitment (and without burning any bridges if you hate the city!).

- **StyleCareers.com,** www.stylecareers.com*
  Excellent site for fashion design positions. It has a searchable database of fashion employers, plus helpful résumé and interview tips.

- **Solomon-Page Group,** spgjobs.com/fashion*
  Fashion postings from Solomon-Page Group, a recruiting service. Primarily focuses on mass market brands.

- ***Women's Wear Daily,*** wwd.com*
  Job opportunities in fashion and related industries. Most positions are based in New York and range from entry level to senior level, across all aspects of the industry. Some listings are viewable with free registration; others require paid subscription.

- **FashionInternships.net**
  Internship listings from over 600 different companies—including

many in PR and marketing. Subscribers pay for access and can apply for internships directly through the site.

DESIGN RESOURCES

- ***20th Century Fashion,*** by Linda Watson, Firefly Books Ltd., 2004
  Chronicles designers, cultural influences, and technological advances through the twentieth century. Indexed both by decade and alphabetically by designer, this is a must-read for anyone interested in fashion history.

- ***Couture Sewing Techniques,*** by Claire B. Shaeffer, Taunton Books, 2001
  A far-from-basic guide to producing flawless hand-stitched garments. Jackets, coats, and eveningwear are emphasized. If you're interested in sewing like they do in the haute couture houses, this is a great reference.

- ***Encyclopedia of Clothing and Fashion*** (three volumes), Valerie Steele, ed., Scribner Library of Daily Life, 2004
  Incredibly wide-ranging encyclopedia with articles on textiles, clothing styles, and construction techniques as well as historical articles on famous designers and stylish fashion influencers. Many articles treat the cultural and social dimensions of fashion, and each entry includes a helpful bibliography. See if you can find this one in your library, since the entire set retails for over $400.

- ***Fairchild Encyclopedia of Fashion Accessories,*** by Phyllis G. Tortora, Fairchild Books and Visuals, 2003
  Broad overview of contemporary fashion accessories and the materials used to produce them. Excellent text for anyone considering accessory design.

- ***Fashion Illustration,*** by Kathryn Hagen, Prentice Hall, 2004
  A book on drawing for fashion designers, written by a fashion illustration professor. Good resource for designers preparing their portfolios for job interviews.

- ***Portfolio Presentation for Fashion Designers,*** by Linda Tain, Fairchild Publications, 2003
  A great guide for anyone considering a fashion design career. The author gives very detailed advice on how to assemble a great portfolio.

- **Pantone,** pantone.com
  The color experts known for their book of colors with formulas, this is a great resource for colorists or anyone interested in developing their color knowledge. Free registration for access to articles.

- ***Patternmaking for Fashion Design,*** 3rd edition, by Helen Joseph Armstrong, Prentice Hall, 2000
  A comprehensive, well-illustrated volume with clear instructions for learning patternmaking.

- ***Saturday Night Hat: Quick, Easy Hatmaking for the Downtown Girl,*** by Eugenia Kim, Potter Craft, 2006
  Patterns and instructions for making 30 different kinds of hats, by celebrity millinery designer (and overnight fashion sensation) Eugenia Kim.

- ***Sew U: The Built by Wendy Guide to Making Your Own Wardrobe,*** by Wendy Mullin, Eviana Hartman, and Beci Orpin, Bulfinch Press, 2006
  A step-by-step sewing guide from the designer behind *Built by Wendy*, complete with patterns and tips on how to customize existing fashions and make them your own.

FASHION BUSINESS RESOURCES

- ***Contemporary Visual Merchandising and Environmental Design,***
  3rd edition, by Jay Diamond and Ellen Daimond, Fairchild Books, 1998
  Describes how to use color, lighting, props, and visual themes to
  generate sales.

- ***The End of Fashion: How Marketing Changed the Clothing Business
  Forever,*** by Teri Agins, HarperCollins, 2000
  A book by a writer from the *Wall Street Journal* looking at the business
  side of fashion design: manufacturing, retailing, and image making.

- ***Fashion: From Concept to Consumer,*** by Gini Stephens Frings,
  Prentice Hall, 2004
  Describes the business side of the industry in detail, with sections
  on color analysis, textile design and manufacturing, and garment
  distribution channels. Frings's book is often used as a textbook in
  "Survey of the Fashion Industry" courses.

- ***Fashion Victim: Our Love-Hate Relationship with Dressing,
  Shopping and the Cost of Style,*** by Michelle Lee, Harper Paperbacks,
  2000
  Humorous and insightful look at how we shop, from a former editor at
  Glamour and *Mademoiselle.*

- ***Why Customers Do What They Do,*** by Marshal Cohen, McGraw-Hill,
  2005
  Written by an expert in consumer behavior and the chief analyst with
  forecasting company NPD Group. This book has great insights on
  branding, marketing, and sales strategies.

- ***Why We Buy: The Science of Shopping,*** by Paco Underhill, Simon and
  Schuster, 1999
  Stories and research about Americans' retail experiences and
  preferences. If you're interested in becoming a merchandiser or you
  plan on working in a clothing store as part of your career strategy,
  this is a good read.

INDUSTRY GLOSSARY

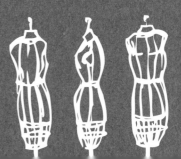

account executive: Salesperson for a fashion company; generally works in a showroom, where they help buyers from various retailers select items for their respective stores.

aesthetic: The overall style and look of a designer's design work, expressive of the designer's sense of what is beautiful.

apparel graphics: Anything printed, sewn, or appliquéd onto clothing, including logos, words, and images.

atelier de couture: Workrooms where designers of *haute couture* work.

better: Refers to labels whose design, cut, and fabric are often better than lower-priced lines, with a price point between $150 and $300.

bridge: Fashions that are one step down in price and exclusivity from designer fashions, with prices from $400 to $600 per piece.

buyer: Retail store representative who purchases merchandise from manufacturers.

CAD (computer-aided design): The use of software programs such as Photoshop, Illustrator, and U4ia for creating textile designs, graphics for fabrics, trims, embroidery, and appliqués.

color correction: Process in which a color specialist compares samples that come back from a dye house against the original color swatch.

color teams: A group of color specialists, often employed by large companies to research trends in color; working closely with the design team, they develop the color palettes and color books for a season.

colorways or **color stories:** The color palette used in a given season.

construction: The sewing and construction of a garment.

contemporary: Refers to trendy but affordable clothing designed primarily for women in their 20s and 30s.

control: The tracking of profits and losses, involving maintenance of various financial records.

copyright: The exclusive rights to use or reproduce a design, image, or written text.

corporation: A highly structured business format with shareholders, stocks, and a board of directors.

cost sheet: Itemizes the costs of the raw materials necessary to produce one unit of product (in the fashion world, that means one garment). For a bathing suit, for example, the cost sheet would include fabric, trim, lining, embellishments, thread, and any hardware (fasteners, buckles, etc.).

costing: Determining the cost of making each garment in a given line.

croquis (CROAK-y)**:** Quick sketches, usually in pencil, that demonstrate design concepts; often collected into a croquis book.

cutter: Person who cuts out material that will then be sewn into garments by other team members.

demicouture: High-end, one-of-a-kind handmade fashions that resemble couture in their construction yet do not meet all criteria necessary for *haute couture* designation.

designer label: Fashions sold at a much higher price point than most labels, often exceeding $1,000 per piece; typically sold in exclusive department stores and boutiques.

diffusion line: Designer's secondary line, sold at a price point that is lower than their haute couture or primary designer line, making the collection more widely accessible.

distress: To make fabric look old and worn out; often used on denim products.

distribution: The process of getting goods ordered by a retail outlet from the production site to a storage warehouse before finally shipping to the stores; often referred to as supply-chain distribution.

draping: Placing and pinning fabric on a mannequin to measure and create a pattern.

dye house: Business that dyes fabric and yarn to its customers' specifications.

embellishments: Anything added to the surface of a garment, including embroidery, appliqués, feathers, and beads; does not include lace (which is considered *trim*) or buttons (which are classified as fasteners).

fit model: Models garments for the designer so that fit can be checked before an order is placed with the manufacturer.

fitting: Process in which a designer reviews the fit of a sample garment, determining what adjustments need to be made before the garment goes into production.

flat sketches: Illustrations that describe the basic shape of the garment.

forecaster—trend or **fashion:** Predicts what styles, colors, and fabrics will be trendy in one to two years; can either work for a fashion house or an independent trend company.

grading (or **pattern grading**): Reproducing patterns for a garment in a range of sizes; now usually done with computers.

gross margin: Gross profit divided by net sales.

gross margin return on investment (GMROI): Gross margin divided by average inventory cost; the higher the GMROI, the happier your bosses.

gross profit: Sales revenue minus the cost of goods (for example, if you sell an item for $100 and the materials, labor, and advertising cost you $10, your gross profit is $90).

hangtag: Tag attached to a garment that includes size and price information.

haute couture: French for "high fashion"; refers to both a very select group of Paris fashion houses and to the clothes those houses produce; one-of-a-kind garments that show exclusively in Paris and are produced by an officially recognized haute couture house (as determined by the French Ministry of Industry).

junior: Clothing designed for girls in junior high and high school.

line: The designs created for a particular season and a particular customer, often developed around a theme that relates the pieces.

line sheets: Detailed reports listing products' wholesale costs, retail costs, colors, and delivery dates.

market week: Period in which new lines are debuted, during which account executives walk clients through the showroom to introduce them to the new fashions for upcoming seasons.

marketing: Developing strategies for promoting, pricing, developing, and distributing products.

mass-market: Refers to clothing that generally sells for less than $50 per piece; often sold at large retailers such as Wal-Mart or Target. Also referred to as budget fashion.

massclusivity: "Exclusivity for the masses"; the creation of products with a luxury or high-end allure for sale to the trend-savvy masses (examples include Stella McCartney's one-time line for H&M or custom-designed Adidas sneakers).

merchandiser: Works across a fashion company's departments to set retail goals, forecast trends, and develop the seasonal line plan (i.e., what's going to be sold in the stores).

moderate: Fashions that are typically mass marketed for the average consumer, are not equated with exclusivity as designer or bridge/better lines can be, and often cost as little as $20 or as much as $120.

mood boards: Collages of photos and fabric samples used as initial inspirations for a line.

open call: An event at which new designers can show their work to buyers from large retail stores, such as Saks.

patternmakers: Professional who takes designer's concepts and interprets them into patterns for the construction of both samples and retail-ready garments.

pitch: A sales presentation to executives of a single concept or entire line.

portfolio: A compilation of a designer's best work.

prêt-a-porter: See *ready-to-wear*.

private label: Fashion lines that large retailers manufacture and sell exclusively in their own stores.

product development team: Strategy team comprising representatives from design, merchandising, and production that determines what products will be designed and created.

production floor: Warehouse-style environment where garments are manufactured.

production manager: Supervises the entire garment production process, overseeing delivery schedules, quality control, cost analysis, and factory performance.

quality control: Checking finished products to ensure that they meet company standards.

ready-to-wear (prêt-a-porter): High-end fashions that are produced in a range of standard sizes, and as such can be worn "off the rack"; unlike haute couture garments, not one-of-a-kind and are thus less expensive.

resort: Apparel season originally intended for rich jetsetters traveling to tropical climates; now worn year-round by a range of customers.

retail merchandiser: Sales professionals who work with buyers to determine the best ways to promote their products.

salon de couture: Haute couture designer's showroom.

sample maker: Creates the first prototype of a designer's garment, usually out of an inexpensive material such as muslin.

samples: Trial garments made to establish the correct fit and fix any issues that may arise during production.

seasons: The divisions of the annual fashion calendar (spring, summer, fall, resort, and winter/holiday); typically designed six months to a year before they are presented.

secondary lines: Lines in a less expensive category, created by designers who already have pricier, more exclusive ready-to-wear lines.

shopping: Studying the market for design inspiration, to see what's being worn and how it's accessorized, and to get a feel for local and international fabrics, colors, and lifestyles.

showroom: Location where the coming season's merchandise is displayed and account managers take orders from store buyers.

sourcing: Determining which textiles and trim will be used for a garment, including how and when they will be delivered; much now done internationally.

spec sheet (or **spec**): Short for "manufacturer's specification sheet"; a detailed description of a garment, including its component pieces, all available colors and sizes, quantities, and production method.

sportswear: Clothing that consists of separate pieces that can be mixed and matched, such as shirts, pants, skirts, and jackets; an American design specialty.

style setups: Detailed sheets on merchandise being carried, color, and pricing information.

stylist: Works with editors, art directors, makeup artists, and photographers to create the right look for photo shoots, ads, editorials, films, movies, and other media.

supply chain: Network through which fashion companies procure raw materials, manufacture garments, and distribute products.

swatching: Cutting clean samples of fabric and trims and cataloging them for future use, along with their fabric content, washing instructions, and cost.

taste level: The price point and level of sophistication evident in a designer's work.

tech packs: Exacting, highly specific documents that explain each element needed for production; sent by designers to factory manufacturers.

technical designer: Takes the fashion designer's concept and interprets it as a design that can be followed by manufacturers.

textile designer: Creates images and patterns for fabrics.

textile mill: Company that constructs knit and woven fabrics.

tracking: The process by which a garment is closely followed through the production process.

trade show: Large events at which companies promote new products to buyers, who are able to review lines from many vendors in a single venue.

trim: Beads, buttons, piping, ribbons, elastic, lace, and embroidery.

trunk show: A mini runway show presenting a traveling selection of a designer clothes, usually conducted in high-end department stores.

tween: Customer between the age of 9 and 12.

visual merchandiser: Arranges clothes on mannequins and in window displays, creating a store's atmosphere.

CAREER-PLANNING WORKBOOK

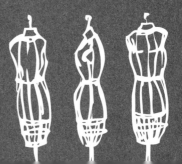

MY CONTACTS

Keep notes about all the people you add to your network—if you're meeting as many people as you should, you won't be able to remember all their details! When you reconnect with someone a few days, weeks, or months after your initial meeting, a brief reminder of where and how you met will make it more likely that you'll get a response. Keep track of the email correspondence you have with these contacts: Start a folder in your email program titled *Job Search*, and stash all your messages there in case you need to refer to them later.

Name: Leah Dente

Company: Mama's (boutique in Brooklyn)

Title/Department: Assistant women's buyer

Where We Met: Jess's graduation party—she's Jess's cousin. I asked her if her pendant was by Me & Ro—it was—and then we chatted about the F.I.T. associate program (She graduated in '03). She told me to call her next time I was in New York

Follow-ups: Sent her a note on 8/15 when I saw Mama's written up in Lucky.

Notes: Get her to review my resume when applying for jobs.

Name:

Company:

Title/Department:

Where We Met:

Follow-ups:

Notes:

Name: _____

Company: _____

Title/Department: _____

Where We Met: _____

_____

Follow-ups: _____

_____

Notes: _____

_____

~~~~~~

Name: _____

Company: _____

Title/Department: _____

Where We Met: _____

_____

Follow-ups: _____

_____

Notes: _____

_____

Name: _____

Company: _____

Title/Department: _____

Where We Met: _____

_____

Follow-ups: _____

_____

Notes: _____

_____

~~~~~~

Name: _____

Company: _____

Title/Department: _____

Where We Met: _____

_____

Follow-ups: _____

_____

Notes: _____

_____

Name: _____

Company: _____

Title/Department: _____

Where We Met: _____

_____

Follow-ups: _____

_____

Notes: _____

_____

～～～～～～～～～～～～～～～～～～～～～～～～～～～～～

Name: _____

Company: _____

Title/Department: _____

Where We Met: _____

_____

Follow-ups: _____

_____

Notes: _____

_____

COMPANY RESEARCH

BONUS TIP: Start a folder on your computer where you store electronic copies of any articles or press releases about the company.

Got an interview coming up? Knock their socks off by showing just how much you know about the company and its projects. After you impress them with your expertise, how could they help but hire you? You can also use these pages to collect research on any companies you'd *like* to be interviewing at someday.

Company: Zeitgeist PR

Contact: Andrew Goldstein, ag@zeitgeist.com (5 years with company)— Tara's friend

History: Founded 10 years ago by two magazine editors who went into PR; they started with just fashion clients, but now also rep a few home and furniture designers

Major Competitors: Su and Partners (similar size and age); Walker Currin (similar kinds of designers)

Significant Projects: Ginny Hall's 2005 airport-themed show and after party

Recent News: They recently expanded and are aggressively recruiting entry-level people

Other Notes: Andrew says that they really like people who know the design field inside out—they always ask interviewees about their favorite magazines, so have some good answers ready*!!!*

Company: _____

Contact: _____

History: _____

_____

Major Competitors: _____

Significant Projects: _____

Recent News: _____

_____

Other Notes: _____

_____

~~~~~~~~~~~~~~~~~~~~~~~~~~~~~~~~~~~~~~

Company: _____

Contact: _____

History: _____

_____

Major Competitors: _____

Significant Projects: _____

Recent News: _____

_____

Other Notes: _____

_____

Company: _____

Contact: _____

History: _____

_____

Major Competitors: _____

Significant Projects: _____

Recent News: _____

_____

Other Notes: _____

_____

~~~~~~

Company: _____

Contact: _____

History: _____

_____

Major Competitors: _____

Significant Projects: _____

Recent News: _____

_____

Other Notes: _____

_____

RÉSUMÉ WARM-UP

List the classes, jobs, and experiences you've had that demonstrate your proficiency in the following areas. (For more specific guidelines, see Chapter 3. Remember, your experiences don't all have to be industry-related! During your three years as a customer service rep at the Apple store, you learned valuable people and communication skills that can transfer to any job.

On the following pages, write down whatever you can think of, even if you're not entirely sure it's applicable. You can always choose to focus on certain jobs and experiences when you actually write your résumé.

Creative Skills

_____

_____

_____

_____

_____

_____

_____

_____

_____

_____

_____

Computer/Technical Skills

Business Skills

_____

_____

_____

_____

_____

_____

_____

_____

_____

_____

_____

_____

_____

_____

_____

People Skills

Organizational/Office Skills

_____

_____

_____

_____

_____

_____

_____

_____

_____

_____

_____

_____

_____

_____

_____

_____

_____

RÉSUMÉ ACTION WORDS

Your résumé is a marketing tool, so strive to make it a compelling advertisement for yourself. After you've written down all your relevant experience, use the list of keywords below to make your work sound as active and impressive as possible (without lying, of course!).

Also make sure to break down your job into specific duties. Rather than just listing "Camp Counselor" on your résumé and calling it a day, take a few extra minutes to articulate everything you were responsible for: *Supervised thirty 10–12-year-olds; coordinated daily swim sessions and sports events; developed three-month leadership program for older students; wrote weekly newsletter for parents.*

accelerated	designed	led	reorganized
activated	devised	maintained	reported
adapted	directed	managed	represented
administered	documented	mastered	researched
analyzed	drafted	maximized	responsible
applied	edited	modeled	reviewed
approved	eliminated	modified	revised
arranged	established	motivated	scheduled
assembled	evaluated	negotiated	set up
assisted	examined	operated	shaped
built	executed	organized	simplified
compiled	expanded	overhauled	solicited
completed	facilitated	oversaw	solved
composed	formulated	participated	streamlined
conceived	founded	performed	structured
conceptualized	generated	planned	supervised
conducted	guided	prepared	supported
consolidated	handled	presented	surveyed
constructed	illustrated	produced	synthesized
consulted	implemented	programmed	taught
contributed	improved	promoted	tested
controlled	increased	proposed	trained
coordinated	initiated	proved	translated
created	interacted	publicized	utilized
critiqued	interpreted	published	volunteered
delegated	introduced	recommended	worked
developed	launched	reduced	wrote

INTERVIEW WARM-UP

During your interviews, it's pretty much guaranteed that the following questions will pop up—a lot. So prepare your answers now, before you're in the hot seat.

Tell me about yourself.

_____

_____

_____

_____

_____

Make sure you tailor your answers to the specific company you're interviewing for!

Why do you want to go into the fashion industry?

_____

_____

_____

_____

_____

What do you know about our company?

_____

_____

_____

_____

Why do you want to work at this company?

_____

_____

_____

_____

Who are some of your favorite designers? Why?

_____

_____

_____

_____

What are your strengths?

_____

_____

_____

_____

What are your weaknesses?

_____

_____

_____

When and how do you do your best work?

_____

_____

_____

_____

_____

Tell me about a time when you had to overcome a difficult situation.

_____

_____

_____

_____

_____

What inspires you?

_____

_____

_____

_____

_____

Tell me about your internships.

_____

_____

_____

_____

_____

_____

Where do you see yourself in five years?

_____

_____

_____

_____

_____

_____

Do you have any questions for me?

_____

_____

_____

_____

_____

_____

Your 5 Talking Points

Interviews often go by in a big blur, and 30 minutes later you're standing in the lobby thinking, *What just happened?* Learn from the politicians: Before you walk into an interview, think of the five things you most want to emphasize. Maybe it's the fact that you handled a full courseload while juggling two part-time jobs. Maybe it's the fact that you wrote your senior essay on the impact the company has had on the industry. Maybe it's the great transferable skills you gained by volunteering at the animal shelter. Whatever they are, note them here. But don't go crazy and list everything impressive about yourself! Force yourself to focus on the most important things.

1. _____

2. _____

3. _____

4. _____

5. _____

Your 30-Second Biography

Sometimes, you don't get much time to make a big impression. Can you paint a vivid, compelling portrait of yourself in less than a minute? Write your 30-second biography in the space below. Memorize it. Use it.

_____

_____

_____

_____

INTERNSHIP TRACKING SHEET

Date	Company	Department	Contact Name	Contact Info	Reference Name	Activity	Next Step

JOB SEARCH TRACKING SHEET

Date	Company	Department	Contact Name	Contact Info	Reference Name	Activity	Next Step

ABOUT THE AUTHORS

Angie Wojak is the Director of Career Services at Parsons the New School for Design, where for the past nine years she has worked with alumni and employers to connect student designers with career opportunities. Angie is a graduate of the School of Visual Arts and the University of Missouri-Columbia, where she received her MFA in Fine Arts. Before joining Parsons, she taught drawing, printmaking, and design courses at Lincoln University and the University of Missouri and was a lecturer at the Museum of Modern Art.

Marianne Hudz is an executive search consultant with Edward W. Kelley and Partners. She was the Founding Director of Career Services at Otis College of Art and Design in Los Angeles, where she worked extensively with the School of Fashion Design. A native Angeleno, she holds a bachelor's degree from Occidental College. Marianne lives with her husband, Tony, and probably has the smallest closet of anyone who's ever written about fashion.

ACKNOWLEDGMENTS

Special thanks to our patient and hardworking editor at Spark Publishing, Nina Shen Rastogi, for her expert guidance (and excellent sense of humor!) throughout the writing process. Thanks too to Kathy Schreiner for carefully reviewing the final manuscript and offering valuable feedback. Much appreciation to Rod Berg, Krysta Vollbrecht, Angela Tsuei, Emily Campbell, Junko Carter, Erica Sewell, James Mendolia, Tom Handley, Alva Hazell, Elizabeth Benator, Barbara Knapp, Miguel Cruz, Carmela Spinelli, Daisy Lewellyn, Adam Reiter, Kathy Van Ness, Michael Fuller, John Bernards, and Roberta Pasciuti for their guidance and inspiration, and to the many fashion industry professionals who contributed their advice, quotes, and experiences to this book. Thank you to our families (Joe Wojak, Troy Pannell, Eric Pannell, Tony Hudz, Andrea King, Amy Martin, and Jason and Katie Odden) for their unconditional support and a summer of Sundays without us. We'd like to dedicate this book to our parents, Lester and Charlene Pannell and George King, and to the memory of Virginia King.